Route 66

Also by Tom Snyder

Pacific Coast Highway Traveler's Guide

When You Close Your Eyes

The Two-Lane Gourmet

Route 66
Traveler's Guide and Roadside Companion

4th Edition

Tom Snyder

St. Martin's Griffin ⚞ New York

Note to the Reader

You will notice a few advertisements from the 1930s scattered throughout this guide. Although none of these businesses are to be found along the highway today, the ads provide something of the charm and allure of way-back-then travel over Route 66.

Further, in unsettled times, many small businesses both on and off Route 66 are struggling for survival and renovation projects have been slowed or halted, while others have not yet begun. As a result, it cannot be stated with certainty which of these will be part of your journey. Where an attraction is in doubt, you'll find its present circumstances noted in the book. So discover all you can and keep a good thought for those who carry on.

ROUTE 66 TRAVELER'S GUIDE AND ROADSIDE COMPANION. Copyright © 2000, 2006, 2011 by Thomas J. Snyder. All rights reserved. Printed in the United States of America. For information, address St. Martin's Press, 175 Fifth Avenue, New York, N.Y. 10010.

www.stmartins.com

ISBN 978-0-312-64425-3

10 9 8 7 6 5 4

This one is for Roger

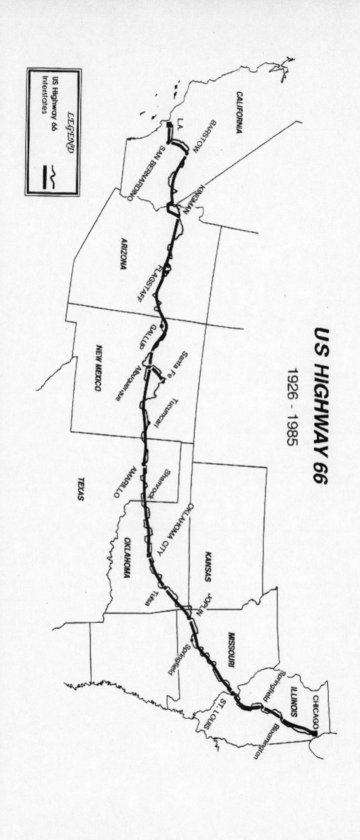

US HIGHWAY 66

1926 - 1985

LEGEND

US Highway 66
Interstates

CONTENTS

ACKNOWLEDGMENTS

This latest edition of the *Route 66 Traveler's Guide and Roadside Companion* benefited from the foresight and unflagging support of its editor, Daniela Rapp, and of the stand-up crews in art and production at St. Martin's Press. All have helped the work live up to its subject.

When all-new digital maps were needed, Dr. Jill Saligoe-Simmel, codeveloper of Ortelius, the mapping software used here, lent her technical and personal support to an author struggling with details. Jim Powell provided exhaustive information about Route 66. And when a new digital master was also needed, Jim was our go-to guy, delivering a scanned and formatted version of the last edition in a matter of hours.

Thanks go also to those road warriors who contributed time and mileage, phone-camera images, and information about the road from Chicago to Santa Monica. They suggested—and we've all agreed—that this edition should recognize individuals who have supported the renaissance of Route 66 for over twenty years. So here we credit those who have gone before as well as those who soldier on, making every bend in the road more exciting and homecomings all the warmer.

At the close of World War II, Jack Rittenhouse and Bobby Troup both crossed the country, each contributing his version of a guide to Route 66. Forty years later, a new chapter opened for a national icon that some intended to bury. Author Michael Wallis wrote the first luggage-size book about the road and packed it with colorful landscapes and characters.

Yet, well before the rest of us showed up, Bart Ripp of *The Albuquerque Tribune* was writing the history of the road, its calamities, and enduring value. Partners Jim Ross and Jerry McClanahan were early to document the highway, as was writer Tom Teague. Author-photographer Shellee Graham embroidered the Route 66 experience in her intimate portraits, Donna Tamburelli of the American Association of State Highway and Transportation Officials served up the factual basis of the road's many alignments, and Richard Weingroff of the Federal Highway Administration was an invaluable source of research, articles, and road facts.

Early on, Jim Powell founded the Route 66 Association of Missouri and began creating a detailed history of the road, while Freeman McCullah of the Missouri Department of Transportation showed what could be accomplished with the leadership of state highway officials. Mike Pitel brought New Mexico's beauty and breadth to the forefront for travelers seeking the spirit of Route 66 in the American West.

Some served the road as critical needs arose. During a lengthy changing of the guard at the Santa Fe Railway's La Posada property in Winslow, Arizona—now one of the most celebrated of all the Harvey Houses—Janice Griffith of the Old Trails Museum once strung together five hundred feet of garden hose, reaching from her home all the way down to the landscaping of the then-battered hotel, to keep it green until help arrived in the form of Allan Affeldt and Tina Mion, who not only restored the hotel but managed to bring it to a state surpassing its former glory.

Still others became part of the Route 66 legend. Travelers' experience was made more special by Ramona Lehman, who preserved and is constantly upgrading the Munger Moss Motel in Lebanon, Missouri. Fran Hauser and Joann Harwell have saved the Midpoint Café in Adrian, Texas, from certain doom and made it an apple-pie centerpiece for Route 66 today.

None of this could have been done without the able cheerleading abilities of road fans such as Angel Delgadillo, Bob Waldmire, and Winslow's golden girl, Diane Patterson. Whether traveling the highway or welcoming others in from it, they turned a dim future into light.

Through their constant hearts, all the gentle people mentioned here have championed the road's future and helped secure it so you can enjoy your journey, and writer-producer and Oscar nominee John Lasseter could one day create *Cars,* a brilliant story through which the road and its special places reached a whole new generation of Route 66 fans.

Thank you all.

An iconic old highway—one that represents what is good about America—is in your debt.

WELCOME TO THE OLD ROAD

Traveling is about seeing new places and about pointing a camera at squinting people or objects that usually turn out to be too far away.

Traveling is about spending money on stuff you'd never dream of buying at home. It's about discovering the different and occasionally the bizarre—about finding something adventurous, daring, and even romantic in yourself. It's about widening your horizons along with the changing view beyond the windshield.

Traveling is like racy lingerie, trashy magazines, kitchen gadgets, and auto accessories. None of these are necessary, but they all make life a little more interesting, a little spicier than it might otherwise be. Old Route 66 is like that. No longer necessary to efficient cross-country travel, the road has been replaced by seamless interstate highways with no stoplights, no places of special interest, no appealing monstrosities—just mile-by-mile progress. After a time the ordinariness of it all is like watching a computer screen saver.

But Route 66? Ah, Route 66 was never ordinary. From its commissioning in 1926, as the first highway to link Chicago with Los Angeles, US 66 was, to townspeople along the route and travelers alike, something special. Soon it was even being called the most magical road in all the world. And by any standard, that's what it became.

Swinging southwest by west from Lake Michigan, US 66 crossed the rivers, plains, mountains, deserts, and canyons of eight states and several Native American nations before ending—2,448 miles later—on a corner near the Pacific. Yet like most American highways of the day, the original roadway remained little more than a dusty transcontinental rut that usually filled with water and mud at the least occasion of rain. Records make it clear that Lindbergh's 1927 solo flight over the Atlantic was easier than a cross-country trek by automobile in the same year. Travelers who made it as far as the Great Mojave paid dearly to load their vehicles onto railroad flatcars rather than risk a breakdown out on the vast desert.

Welcome to the Old Road

Still, the road that became the Main Street of America was nothing if not commercially inspired. As a result of an intense lobbying effort by the U.S. 66 Highway Association, a patchwork of farm-to-market roads and old trails was transformed into a single all-weather highway. More important, the association transformed Route 66 into something else as well: an extraordinary experience—*a destination in itself.* A few days' travel on Route 66 became a tour of the highway and the excitement of being on the road became as important as any destination. In advertising terms, that's when the sizzle caught up with the steak.

By the mid-1930s, the highway was creating its own myth, growing larger than life. It soon became *the* way west. First it was John Steinbeck, who recognized a feminine, nurturing quality in Route 66 and termed it "the mother road," forever embedding the highway and the Joad family in the nation's consciousness. After World War II, it was Bobby Troup's turn. His musical TripTik for getting your kicks on Route 66 has since been recorded by nearly everyone from the Andrews Sisters to the Rolling Stones, Depeche Mode, and Tom Petty. But it was the first great recording by Nat King Cole that changed the way an entire nation would pronounce the name. After Cole's cover of the song, it would be "root sixty-six" forever.

During the 1960s, the road earned top billing in the literate and successful TV series *Route 66,* propelled across the continent by Nelson Riddle's magnificent road theme.

In the process, US 66 became much more than a highway. For the millions who traveled her (and the millions more who want to), the road was transformed from a concrete thoroughfare into a national symbol: a vital life-sign for us all. A pathway to better times—seldom found, but no less cherished. Route 66 came to represent not only who we were as a people, but who we knew we could be. Not a bad thing to find in a road.

Yet change came to old Route 66, as to all who traveled her. Abandoned in many places, she was reduced to the homely duties of a "frontage road" in others. Her poetic double digits were assigned to an interstate near Washington, D.C.; her job was taken over by a homogenized, fast-food freeway. With the final stretch of I-40 opened in 1984, and the decision by state transportation officials to remove all traces of Route US 66, the upbeat road rhythms became a dirge. And this time we risked losing a great deal more than just another highway: this time we were in danger of losing something of great value in ourselves.

But there ought to be a saying that you can't keep a good road down. You can take away her destination, even steal her magic numbers. But you can't keep old Route 66 out of the hearts and memories of a succession of generations of roadborne Americans.

Just by driving the old road and visiting with the wonderful people to be found along the way, you'll become part of the spirit and the legacy of Route 66 across America. As you follow the updated road maps in this book, you'll find the thin, wavy line that was once Route 66 is often cut to pieces by the double-barreled interstate. But much of it is still there.

And there's a lot of fire and an embracing warmth in the grand old lady. If anything, Route 66 is even more exciting today. When you regain something once feared lost, the sentiment is sweeter by far.

So take in everything, experience the road fully, be a part of what you find. Enjoy every curve, every place to stop along the way. Re-create for yourself and share with those you love the sweetness of a time gone by—a time still to be found on the Main Street of America. Welcome to the old road.

Welcome to Route 66.

USING THESE UPDATED MAPS

Every map in this edition is entirely new, and each has been created from the best sources of information available for various Route 66 alignments. Purists will notice that some sections of the highway's many alignments are not included. In most cases these sections are of secondary interest. Often they are barricaded, in ruin, or on private land. Wherever possible, the focus is on original alignments rather than segments since termed *historic*—especially as may be listed for interstate highways that had nothing to do with Route 66, other than passing in the same general direction.

Please note that the scale of these maps for the route varies. Chicago and other cities are shown in greater detail. But longer sections of open road are compressed. Often the bones of old Route 66 are buried beneath an interstate's eastbound lanes. Sad, I know. Just be happy that so much of the old road is still out there to drive and remember.

These newer maps are as uncluttered as possible. Yet adding up mileage on a map is no fun. So a **Route 66 Mileage Table**—on the last pages of the book—puts all those numbers in one place for an easier way to know where you are and the distance ahead to the next town. This table is useful for eastbound travelers as well as those headed west.

A preferred route will always be shown as a dashed line—similar to the blacktop you see through your windshield—so you can always get a quick fix on it with any of the forty-three maps and insets you'll find in this book. Most often, this path will also be one of the original Route 66 alignments. Optional routings are shown with a lighter dashed line. For a summary, refer to the Map Symbols on the following page.

As you plan your tour of the old road, it's best to remember that these Route 66 maps are more than commercial maps. They are *illustrated history*. So more than one alignment of the old road, from the 1920s through the 1950s, may appear on a single panel. Each era added

66 Map Symbols

▬ ▬ ▬	66 Preferred Route
⌐⌐⌐⌐	66 Optional Route
▪▪▪▪▪	66 Gravel / Dirt Section
➤➤➤	66 Derelict / Private Section
▬▭	66 Co-Signed Interstate
═══	Other Interstate / Parkway
▬▬	Other Street or Highway
▪▪▪▪▪	66 Bike / Walkway
╫╫╫╫	Railway – Active
╨╨╨╨	Railway – Abandoned
XXXXXX	Bridge – Classic Truss Style
══╲	Bridge – Contemporary
⌐▬▭	River / Dry Wash

its own ingredients to the blend of achievement, despair, and joy that characterized Route 66.

One last note: Being lost from time to time is part of the worth in any journey. Here are two thoughts that may help you balance your time on the road.

Maps are wondrous. They guide us, defy us, and sometimes lead us to what we might have missed, had we followed them precisely.

—Gabrielle Antonini

The Journey is the thing.

—Homer

Remember, too, that Route 66 came to life in pieces and is now traveled in the same way. There's a special symmetry in that.

PLANNING YOUR ROUTE 66 TOUR

If you're one of the many who are tired of the interstate grind, this guide will introduce you to easy-on, easy-off sections of old Route 66. At first you may have only a little time to spare. That's fine. But if you love the feel of an old two-lane road, if you want the experience of going back to an earlier time, if you are like the rest of us—travelers who have become enchanted by Route 66—you'll soon be back for the whole tour. In the meantime, it's always fun to do a little traveling in your mind.

This guide was not designed for coffee-table conversation, however. It will serve you best when kept in the glove compartment or close at hand. It should be well thumbed, brown edged, and stained with juices from your favorite Route 66 cafés and barbecue joints. When the pages get really bad, just have the whole thing bronzed. It might be a good way to memorialize all your experiences along the old road.

Note: Before starting your Route 66 journey, take time to view at least a few sections of the highway from one of the satellite cameras a hundred miles above the earth. East of Alanreed, Texas, for example, satellite photographs show the old dirt section of Route 66, along with the land-hugging curves of earlier tracks and the now-abandoned Rock Island Line roadbed. It's a fascinating look into the past. The same is true across much of the country. In the Arizona and California deserts, the surface comes alive with kaleidoscopic colors seldom visible from road level. Even a few minutes with these images will alter your experience of the drive.

Most-Asked Questions

Which seasons are best? Unless you are pressed by school or work schedules to travel only in summer, you'll enjoy your tour much more during other seasons. October and November are usually wonderful months to travel through the Southwest, with only a small risk of early storms in the Midwest. If you're westbound, that's usually no problem. March through May are also lovely most anywhere along the route. Winter too is a great time to get out of the Snow Belt and experience the change from midwestern temperatures to the sunny, uncrowded beaches of Southern California. Except for the low deserts, where seasonal travel is reversed, discounts of 20 to 25 percent are common for the off-season period from October through April.

Is it safe? The answer is that Route 66 is as safe today as it was some years ago. For the most part, it is a highway of small towns and open land and we've heard of no incidents involving travelers. Just observe normal precautions—especially in cities—and enjoy your tour.

What about facilities en route? There are no known problems. Even on the long northern swing away from the interstate in Arizona, the old route is open but rarely desolate. Food, fuel, accommodations, and other services are usually nearby.

Which direction is best? Plan to drive the highway from east to west if at all possible. Due to the western migration of the American population and the lure of Southern California over the past eighty years or so, Route 66 is primarily a westbound road. Moreover, because travelers were all spent out by the time they returned east, most tourist businesses and attractions are positioned toward westbound traffic with that in mind. Even the chapters of most bidirectional guides are arranged from east to west, so authors and publishers generally present a westbound point of view. Drive other great highways east. But follow Route 66 west!

How many days will it take? Because everyone's touring style is different, there can be no single answer. But here are some handy guidelines. With only brief detours, figure the distance to be 2,400 to 2,600 miles. With a little weather and a surprise or two, driving time will be about eight days—a bit fast for sightseeing. Finally, add two days for the leg up through Santa Fe, a visit to the Grand Canyon, or some beach time along the Pacific Coast Highway. That's eight to fourteen days. If you're aboard a motorcycle, figure about 250 to 300 miles per day. The point is, you'll work it out and have a great time.

How much should I pack? A Route 66 tour is simplicity itself, yet travelers tend to carry enough stuff to outfit a small country. Unless you know you're invited to a maharaja's reception, leave evening and business apparel home. I carried a navy blazer along on half a dozen crossings and never wore it once. Fresh shirts? Buy some Route 66 T-shirts when yours get kinda whiffy. Coin-op laundries are usually available in motels or nearby.

Of course some people just need to fill up a car. My family did. We followed the golden rule of traveling: Be sure you have enough—take too much. Now I generally tour the whole country with one camera and a gym bag. It makes quiet, second-floor rooms a lot easier to reach.

Will I need other maps? Yes. These maps are specialized and local to Route 66. To gain perspective on a day's drive or your entire journey, it's always best to have a set of maps covering the eight states through which Route 66 passes. My first rule of travel is: There is no such thing as having too much fuel or too many maps. A more adventurous view is, that by knowing what may be near by, you stand a better chance of finding places that will become lifetime memories. Go for it!

Remember, too, that dependence on toll-free reservations and such can deaden the feeling of adventure, romance, and personal discovery that comes with exploring a two-lane highway on your own. Let yourself be surprised at where you stay the night.

The aim of this guide is to achieve a balance between touring commentary and your absolute right to find your own way, celebrate your own discoveries, and choose when you need to make time on the interstate—and when you don't.

Even if you're a closet roadie, you'll be delighted to know that, with few exceptions, old Route 66 can still carry you from the edge of Lake Michigan to the California coast. Most of the towns and much of the original roadway remain, and you'll enjoy seeing the country as you may never have seen it before. You'll also enjoy meeting many of the people who have made this highway their life. They're good folks.

Be sure to say hello for all of us.

TRAVELER'S
GUIDE

ILLINOIS

It's tempting to think of old Route 66, stretching from Chicago to Los Angeles, as a happy accident. After all, her famous double-sixes were little more than that, the road having first been designated Route 60. But the truth is that there is a strong Illinois–California connection that predates the road, extending back to the early 1900s, when the route that was to become US 66 was cobbled together from existing pathways. And they really were little more than pathways. Trails, traces, fence-row tracks, farm-to-market roads, and even some private drives were linked with stagecoach routes farther west to create something resembling a continuous roadway—just in time for the unending stream of Tin Lizzies being mass-produced by Henry Ford.

Business and personal connections between Chicago and Los Angeles were already established as well. One of Hollywood's very first moviemakers came not from New York,

but from Chicago. The harsh early winter of 1907 threatened to run Francis Boggs's tiny film company out of business. Only the interior scenes of Boggs's twelve-minute epic,
The Count of Monte Cristo, had been shot when the snows
ended any hope of outdoor filming. Boggs, his crew, and
his players headed west in search of better conditions and
a light more suited to the slow film speeds of the day. They
found what they needed in Los Angeles—bright sunshine,
cheap land, and free scenery.

The following year Boggs moved production to the West
Coast for good. Vitagraph, Mack Sennett, Cecil B. DeMille,
and others followed, of course, but Chicagoan Boggs led the
way. Even the name *Hollywood* came not from the holly trees
that were planted later, but from an upstate neighborhood
in Illinois.

Of the midwestern states, Illinois has always been the
champion trader, track layer, and road builder. With Chicago at its hub—importing and exporting anything mov-
able, anything conceivable—Illinois stole a march on the
East. But Chicago need never have been lured into the trap
of comparison. Better to be called Windy City than Second City. For there is nothing second-class about Chicago.
Its outrageous blend of southern black cool, northern lib-
eralism, and blue-collar ethic, along with its midwestern
reserve and commercial might, is sometimes politically
awkward but always lively.

None can fan the twin flames of devotion and despair
quite like the Cubbies. And even Green Bay cannot match
the chill factor at Soldier Field during a Bears losing streak.
Chicago has exported broad-shouldered poetry, prairie
architecture, miles of unfortunate hams, a large part of
the original cast of *Saturday Night Live,* plus—bet you didn't
know this—the Lava Lite, premier icon of mid-1960s
plastic.

These are good things to know, if you're starting out
on a tour of old Route 66 from its beginning. For Los
Angeles could not have been successfully linked with the
eastern seaboard. Even with today's bicoastal management
style, Southern California and New York have too little in
common. Only Chicago—hunkered down smack in the
middle of America's heartland—could anchor one end
of a great new westering highway that factory workers,

farmhands, hitchhikers, businesspeople, teachers, truckers, and screenwriters would know as their own.

Chicago was, and is, exactly the right place to start.

Chicago to Bloomington

First let's clear up some confusion about the origin of the highway in downtown Chicago. Old Route 66 originally began on Jackson Boulevard at Michigan Avenue, a few blocks north of the present-day departure of Interstate 55 from I-90 and 94. After the 1933 World's Fair provided reclaimed land, the terminus was moved east to Lake Shore Drive at the entrance to Grant Park. Then, in 1955, Jackson Boulevard became an eastbound one-way thoroughfare with Adams Street as its westbound counterpart, one block farther north. So the most direct route west is now via the newer Adams alignment.

But don't let the adventure begin without giving yourself a send-off celebration and a good meal. The best place for both is Lou Mitchell's at 565 W. Jackson Boulevard, where they serve breakfast all day, and still give free Milk Duds to each woman customer. This spot has been a well-loved Chicago landmark since 1923 and has remained unchanged here on the route since 1949. They're open from 5:30 A.M. until 3:00 P.M., and you can even squeeze in a few minutes early to get a running start on your first day out.

Lou Mitchell's is superbly managed, with an atmosphere that is born of both city business and the open road ahead. So bring your maps and guide, find a spot of your own, and be glad that such traditions remain.

It's easy to reach Lou Mitchell's from westbound Adams. Simply turn south on Des Plaines just before the interstate overcrossing, and double back east on Jackson. The restaurant is at Jefferson, with free parking usually available until eight in the morning. And save a Danish for me, okay? We'll be on the road together for 2,400 miles and the bakery here is terrific.

As you go west on Adams, Ashland Avenue will be your heads-up for a turn southwest onto Ogden Avenue through **Cicero**. Ogden is quite a long run through the city, with three jogs along the way. At the first jog just two blocks after Kostner Avenue, be sure to follow Ogden west after exiting the rail undercrossing. Second, a jog through **Lyons**, is detailed on the inset (circle) map following. Third, beyond Lyons is what could become a permanent detour, due to erosion too close to the old road. It's represented on the map; just follow directional signs as posted.

Once a home away from home for Chicago mobsters, Cicero's streets were honeycombed with tunnels allowing gangsters and bootleggers to move unseen from speakeasy to brothel, with even Eliot Ness and his Untouchables none the wiser. Cicero now works hard to present a squeaky-clean image. But some of the tunnels are still there. Perhaps there's one right under the intersection of Ogden and Cicero Avenues.

After Harlem Avenue, it's best to jog south on Harlem Avenue / SR 43 in Lyons, and swing southwest again on Joliet Road. Old Route 66 lies beneath for the next few miles. But if you're hungry, it's hard to do better than the Del Rhea Chicken Basket, a Route 66 icon for years. Take Exit 274 in Willowbrook and bend north on SR 63 to the first right onto Midway Drive. Continue to a right turn on Quincy Road to 645 Joliet Road.

Continue on to the junction with Bollingbrook Road, as the route becomes SR 53 / Independence Boulevard and passes through **Romeoville**. At the junction with SR 7, the road becomes Broadway Street. Follow it south into **Joliet**. Turn east at the T intersection to cross Ruby Street

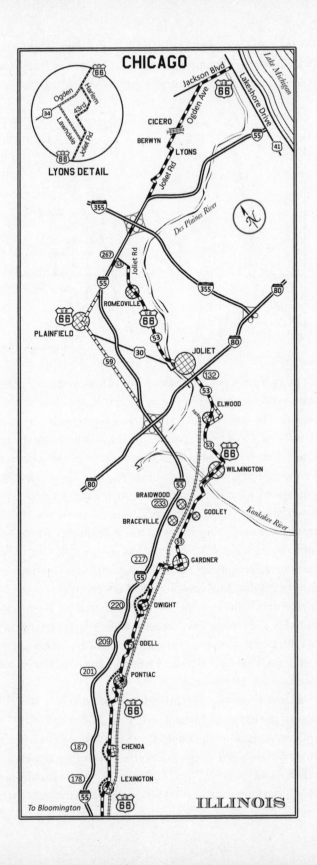

Bridge, and turn south again on Chicago Street. This is the older route and is reminiscent of the lively way that local Route 66 commerce captured the traveler's attention.

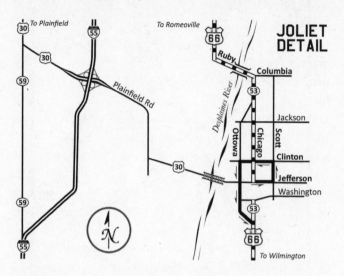

Joliet has become an example for other towns along the way. And along with the gorgeous baroque-style Rialto Square Theater, built in 1926, there's plenty to see. Prison movies or TV series? They've got 'em, with the infamous Old Joliet Prison, once just about the toughest slammer in the country. Antique gasoline pumps? These serve as guideposts for a walking tour through the central area of town. But the village of **Plainfield** is not far behind. Both towns have bragging rights to a confluence of Route 66 and the Lincoln Highway. A few years ago, Plainfield hadn't really caught the Route 66 bug yet, but it's on the way now, with double-sixes sprouting here and there.

For the Plainfield option, continue straight from I-55 onto SR 126 / East Main Street at Exit 261. Turn south on SR 59/Division Street to reconnect with I-55 after about 6 miles. Or take SR 30 from Plainfield southeast into Joliet as a two-for-one route.

Continue to the **Wilmington** exit to rejoin the old route. Just north of Elwood, cross the bridge and at half a mile, jog left, then right onto the old two-lane. Watch for a line of weathered telephone poles—this often signals an older route—and follow Manhattan Road to Mississippi Road, curving back toward SR 53. Around the bend, the two-lane becomes Elwood Road and recrosses the newer highway. Continue west on the old alignment into **El-wood**. Then follow Douglas until it rejoins SR 53 at the southern end of town.

After entering Wilmington, follow the old route west on Baltimore (SR 53) and continue south through **Braid-wood**, **Godley**, and **Braceville**. Some of the first landmarks of old Route 66 appear along this stretch of two-lane highway, along with beer-and-skittles roadhouses. South of **Gardner**, as SR 53 swings back north, make a hard left turn to the south and continue on the old two-lane alignment of Route 66. Or continue south to Bloomington on I-55, which closely parallels this route.

These Illinois villages along old Route 66 are snapshots of a time in America that has all but vanished. Neighbors knew one another and small businesses prospered because they understood local needs—not through mass marketing. So do take time to visit these small towns, where the spirit of Route 66 and a sense of ease live on. A few miles beyond Gardner, **Dwight** is a good introduction. Here, the Texaco/Marathon gas station, dating from 1933, has been lovingly restored and now houses a visitor information center. **Odell** is a variation on the theme, with its 1932 Standard Oil Station—restored by the Illinois Route 66 Association—that lives on as a visitor center. Near **Ca-yuga**, watch for a photo opportunity to the west where, in a cluster of farm buildings, there may still be a barnside ad for Meramec Caverns on Route 66 in Missouri.

From the early days of the old road, Meramec Caverns has been one of the most aggressive and colorful of all highway advertisers. And the cave is a great attraction still, so you might as well start thinking about a stop there. Besides, it's part of traveling to get excited, even to keep asking every few miles if we're *there* yet. You're a card-carrying adult now. You can even stick your feet out of the car window if you want to. Well, for a little while, anyway . . . but leave your socks on.

Running a highway business is no easy task. And life can suddenly seem impossible when the highway department announces that the road will be moved. Some folks fold up and quit while others try to hang on. A few are

able to call on a special form of creativity born of despera-
tion. Near **Pontiac** stands the Old Log Cabin Inn. Actually, it's a slightly newer version. The old inn fronted on
the original Route 66 next to the railroad. But the newer
alignment of the highway was going to pass behind the
place. Even the highway department pitched in and soon
the problem was solved. The entire building was jacked
up, turned around, and plopped down again—facing the
new Route 66.

Lexington offers a wider view of the life and times of
Route 66 in Illinois. Watch for the red neon LEXINGTON
sign erected to pull travelers in from the four-lane bypass.
One section of that bypass has now been closed and re-
dedicated as Memory Lane, a walking trail. That's right,
you can walk right out on a one-mile stretch of the old
pavement, where you'll find period billboards, Burma-
Shave signs, the works.

Continue south and southwest into **Normal** and
Bloomington. Normal dates from a time when women
who wanted to become elementary school teachers—and
were often not welcome at colleges and universities—
attended normal schools. Separatist views waned about
the time Route 66 was certified, and Normal is now the
home of Illinois State University.

As Normal and Bloomington grew, the two cities
merged. Enter Normal on the two-lane, which becomes
Pine, turn south on Linden, west on Willow, and south
again onto Main Street, which slides on down into Bloomington. When Main becomes one-way northbound, follow
US Business 51 south. Turn west at Oakland and south on
Morris, and bear right crossing Six Points Road. Just before the Business Loop, turn right to cross over I-55, then
left to follow Beich Road south from town. If you miss the
turn and end up on I-55, recovery is easy via Exit 154 to
Shirley.

Bloomington to
St. Louis

Heading south toward McLean on the west side of I-55,
be sure to take time for a visit to **Funks Grove**, just

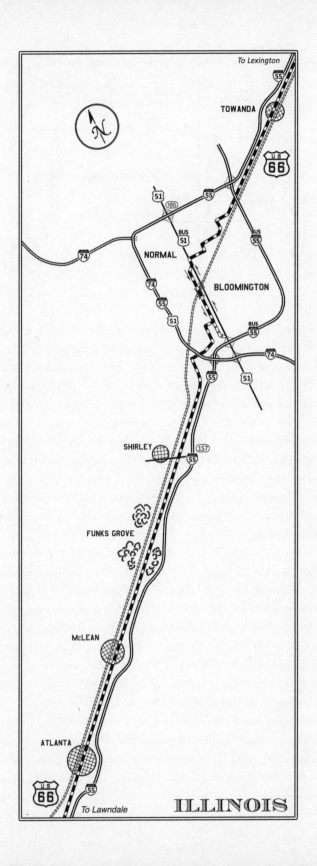

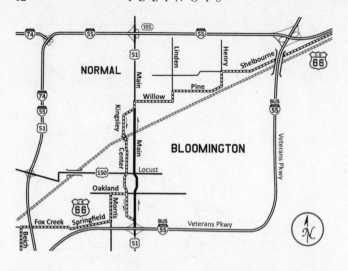

beyond Shirley. Turn west across the tracks for one of the more photogenic spots you'll find on this part of the route. Look over the old railway depot and the antique shop. Then head on across the road and a little south for the famous maple syrup plant. If you're planning to travel this way late in the year, however, you'd best get your reservation in early. The Funks have been making this syrup since the 1800s, so it is quickly sold out. And take it from someone who grew up in sugar bush country, this is *wonderful* maple syrup. What's more, you'll have a little bit of old Route 66 right there in your refrigerator when you get back home.

After passing through **McLean**, follow US 136 west for only a short distance. Watch for the old route angling off to the south toward **Atlanta** and **Lawndale**.

Continue on and enter **Lincoln** via Business Loop 55. Watch for a huge neon palm tree sign on the west side of Lincoln Parkway at SR 10. It's a remnant of the Tropics, a classic 66 joint that may yet be restored. Follow Kickapoo Street to the western jog on Keokuk to Logan, and then onto 5th, Washington, and Stringer. Lincoln is not a big place, so it's fairly easy to get through town. In the Land of Lincoln, this town was the only place to adopt his name *before* he became president. Indeed, the town was actually christened by Lincoln. Still a nice place to raise kids.

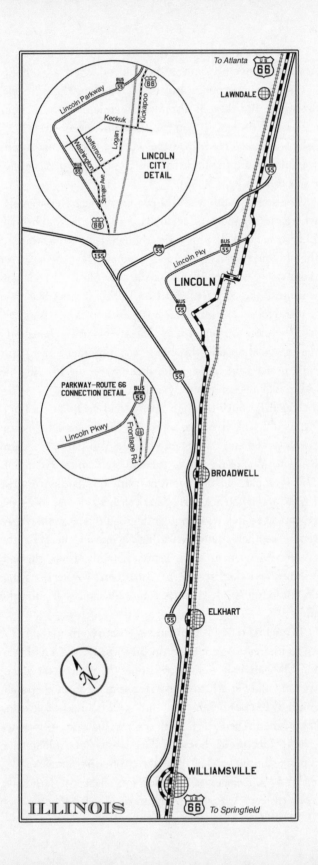

From this point to well beyond Springfield, this is Abraham Lincoln Country. And indeed, there are a number of wonderful public attractions honoring the sixteenth president. But there is also a commercial heaviness about much of it. In fact, if you can find someplace where Lincoln is not advertised to have worked, stayed, or stood, you might want to phone the tourist police with an anonymous tip.

Continuing south, you'll be passing through **Broadwell**, where the remnant of a four-lane is still easiest through **Elkhart** and **Williamsville**, though there are sections of the old, old road along here, if you have the time to ferret them out. South of Williamsville, the old road ends and you must enter **Springfield** on I-55. Take the Sherman exit and follow the interstate business loop, which is mostly old Route 66, through town. There are scattered pieces of the old road around the city—one alignment even runs right under Lake Springfield. If the water level is low, the old roadbed is sometimes visible.

Heading south through Springfield on Business Loop 55, you'll have a choice of routes. You can jog west on South Grand and take MacArthur to Wabash to Chatham Road to Woodside Road, turning south onto old SR 4. This is an old, old alignment of Route 66, dating from the 1920s, and if you are a true fan of early roadbeds, this is the alignment to follow. Although the road is laid out like a series of southerly jumps in a huge game of checkers, the accompanying map is consistent with the route through **Virden** and **Carlinville** to **Staunton**. For sections that do not follow SR 4, Historic Route 66 signs will point the way.

If you find roadside remnants of Route 66 from the 1930s more interesting, continue on Business Loop 55 and take the Chatham exit. Follow old Route 66 on the west side of the interstate south toward **Glenarm**. Continue straight south to the dead end, then onto southbound I-55, exiting at Divernon. There, turn south again on the westside frontage road to **Litchfield**, home of the Ariston Cafe, a long-term roadside business. The Ariston (from the Greek *áristos*, meaning superior) was originally established in Carlinville, along the earliest Route 66 alignment. The family operation

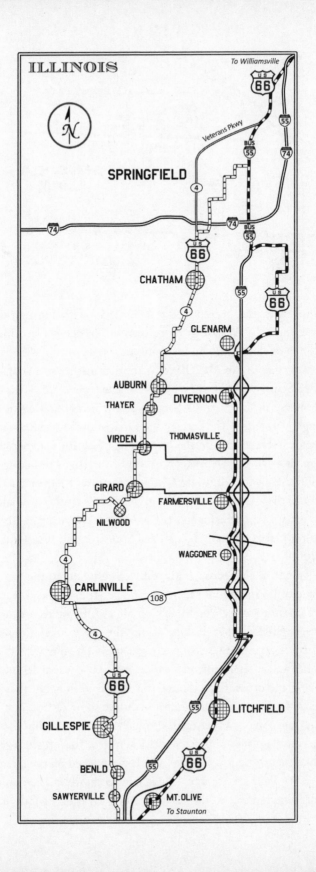

moved to the present location in 1935 with the newer routing. The Ariston is more than an excellent place for lunch or dinner, it's an institution.

Farther on, in **Mt**. **Olive**, is another institution: Souls-by's Service Station at 1st Street, dating from 1926. Henry Soulsby designed the station himself, incorporating de-sign elements of the cottage style that allowed service sta-tions to blend in with the community. Soulsby's soldiered on through the Depression, World War II gas rationing, and the decline of Route 66. Now restored to its original look, the station is one of the great success stories of small business along the highway. The National Register of His-toric Places formally recognized Soulsby's and listed it in 2004.

Continue on through Mt. Olive, recrossing to the west side of I-55 opposite **Stanton**, and go straight ahead. Re-main on the west side to pick up SR 157. If you're passing through **Hamel** at dusk or during the night, a neon cross on a church there helps speed you safely on your way. It's blue and it's big, but most travelers get a warm feeling from the cross. Even though it is rendered in neon, there is something tasteful about it—unlike some of the rotat-ing beacons in Los Angeles, which make their churches resemble places to buy fried chicken. No, this cross is not like that, especially in the rain. It was placed on the front of St. Paul's Lutheran Church by a family whose son drowned at Anzio during the Allied invasion of Italy in

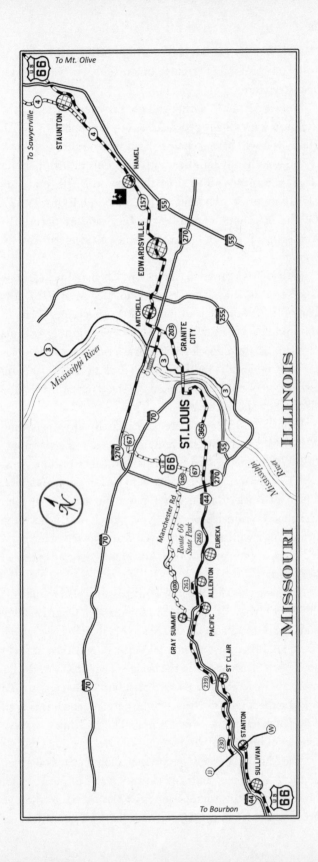

World War II. Clearly advertising nothing, the cross is simply a comforting tribute. In a neighborly way, it says: You Are Here.

Follow SR 157 south through **Edwardsville** to the junction with Chain of Rocks Road, just north of I-270. Here, you will have a choice about which route to follow. If you are already familiar with St. Louis or are short on time, you may wish to skirt the city on I-270, rejoining old Route 66 southbound at the Lindbergh Exit (US 67). Of the old alignments followed by Route 66 across the Mississippi River, only the McKinley Bridge still carries traffic.

Although it's closed to traffic now, Chain of Rocks Bridge is a Route 66 classic and a must-do. Begun in 1927, it is one of the few bridges in the world with a radical bend in the middle. After a checkered history beginning with its closure, Chain of Rocks Bridge was reincarnated as a major link in a walk-and-bike trail. Parking is available on either side of the Mississippi, and a stroll out over the Mississippi is a special treat.

From SR 157, take Chain of Rocks Road west beyond **Mitchell**. At the SR 203 junction, cross to the south side of I-270 following Chain of Rocks Road. Continue west over the ship-canal bridge and on to parking near the river. Chain of Rocks Bridge was repaved for its part in John Carpenter's film *Escape from New York*. It was in fact the bridge over which the patch-eyed Kurt Russell made good his escape and upon which Adrienne Barbeau breathed her bosomy last.

To make the McKinley Bridge crossing, plan to take SR 203 south from Mitchell. Continue through **Granite City** and take Nameoki Road / SR 203 to Madison Avenue, which becomes Broadway Avenue in **Venice**, and then straight across 4th Street and onto the bridge. The McKinley Bridge has been in service for more than a hundred years, so you might expect its deck surface to be derelict, and it was until a recent renovation. Now it's fine. The McKinley is also a marvel of bridge building.

The McKinley crossing is presented on the St. Louis map as the main route, and it is closest to the original. Note, however, that this route requires caution. It passes through areas where it's not good to have a flat, run out of fuel, or drive a convertible with the top down. If this concerns you or time is short, the northern routing—presented as optional—may be a better choice.

Now is a good time to read ahead and plan your crossing.

MISSOURI

Most place names suffer when they are translated from a mother tongue and later contracted. But not Aux Arc, the name of an early Missouri trading post. In the original French, the term is plain. Sensible, like shoelaces. Yet in its modern form, *Ozark* becomes a mythic word. A mystery. Not dark or ominous but a whisper-word full of timeless secrets. The Ozarks. A place of independent people with soft smiles and stout natural reserve—backbone of the Show Me State.

Missourians, hands thrust securely into their pockets, can stand for an hour while they wait for you to state your case, make your best offer, or ask directions. In the end, they'll know all they need to about your business and you'll know nothing more about them than you did an hour ago. Some say that comes naturally to folks of solid mining-farming-mountain stock who had to contend with riverboat gamblers, Damn Yankees, Kansas guerrillas, and the weather hereabouts.

But don't take that to mean that people from Missouri are humorless, for they are not that at all. What other state with heavy investments in manufacturing, shipping, and the aerospace industry declares with a straight face that it is also a world leader in the production of corncob pipes? Where else would you find a county government so fed up with the North–South quarrel over slavery that it refused to stand with either faction and instead formed the completely independent Kingdom of Callaway? And along what other stretch of old Route 66 would you be likely to see a hand-lettered sign advertising GUN & DOG SWAP MEET—WOMEN OK (MAYBE)? Not tongue-in-cheek humor exactly, but sly. Very sly.

The larger part of Missouri hangs suspended between its two major cities, St. Louis and Kansas City. Both these cities have dithered over the years, each feeling at various times inferior, each courting greatness, yet often shrinking from the self-surgery that greatness can require. Through this try-and-try-again atmosphere, old Route 66 plunges diagonally across the state, following the course of the Osage Trail, the Kickapoo Trace, and later, the Federal Wire Road, south and west toward Kansas and Oklahoma. And far beyond.

Perhaps more than any other state through which Route 66 passes, Missouri is a region of great contrasts. Something of the spirit of Mark Twain's *Tom Sawyer* and Harold Bell Wright's *The Shepherd of the Hills* is still present here, along with the torment of civil and border wars. Yet there is also a lingering sense of willing endurance as once embodied in Pony Express riders and the redoubtable Charles Lindbergh.

With Route 66, Missouri has always taken the lead. The Route 66 State Park and a pair of Route 66 Welcome Centers along I-40 are exemplary. And as this is being written, the state has completed a major upgrade in signage, putting up over 750 new signs with directional arrows and the years any given section was in service as Route 66. Look for blue Byway signs on the road as well as the more familiar brown-and-white signs on city streets.

Yet, at a loss for ways to represent the land and culture and people in a single slogan for tourists, the state's department of tourism cried uncle. "Come to Missouri," they finally wrote. "There's no state quite like it." True enough. In spring, when the dogwood is in flower, St. Peter is said to lock heaven's gates so that Ozark souls do not return to a place of greater beauty.

So if tree-shaded main streets full of memories of old Route 66 are your interest, if you are an antiquer and a general poker-about, or if you simply want to cruise over smooth roller-coaster hills, be sure to take a little extra time in Missouri. There *is* no other place quite like it.

St. Louis to Waynesville

Old Route 66 alignments through St. Louis are plentiful but serpentine. If you wish to skirt the city on I-270 to the north, you'll still have an opportunity to follow an

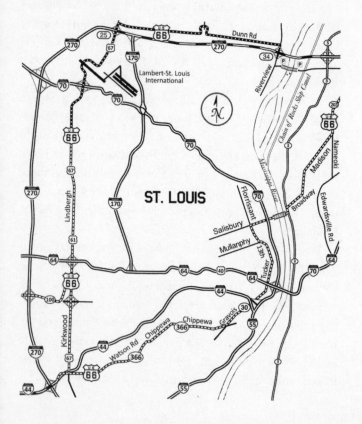

alignment dating from from the 1930s, on Dunn Road— just north of I-270—from Riverview Drive to Lindbergh Boulevard / US 67.

At Lindbergh, a turn south will take you through **Kirkwood** to (New) Watson Road. The traffic is not heavy over this section except during rush hours, and Kirkwood is a charming community with much of the feeling of an earlier time preserved. Look for the railroad depot—a classic and still in service with Amtrak—on the west side just beyond Argonne Drive. And if you've an eye for trains and steam locomotives, there are some splendid displays at the National Museum of Transportion, just a few minutes away. The museum is a mile or so west of I-270, on Barrett Station Road between Dougherty Ferry Road and Big Bend Road.

Dating from the late 1800s to the final days of steam after World War II, the locomotives here range from early pufferbellies to a giant Santa Fe 2-10-4, which once offered Route 66 drivers the chance to race against a truly fast freight highballing through the West ("Faster, Daddy, faster . . .") where the old road often runs right alongside the rifle-shot tracks of the former Atchison, Topeka and Santa Fe. There are lots of other exhibits, too, but the great iron horses steal the show—unless a unit of Coral Court, world famous for its Streamline Moderne design and locally known as a sin-at-noon palace, goes from a shell to fully reconstructed at the museum by the time you visit.

From the museum, an easy way to rejoin the route is by taking I-270 south to Watson Road and merging onto westbound I-44.

If you plan on taking the McKinley Bridge crossing, you'll have a perfect opportunity to visit the Jefferson National Expansion Memorial Gateway Arch, co-located with several excellent museums, historic buildings, and riverfront attractions.

For that crossing, exit from the western end of the McKinley deck, angle over I-70 onto Salisbury Street, turn south on Florrissant Street, and angle left onto Mullanphy Avenue for a quick turn onto North 13th Street. Jog left as 13th Street becomes North Tucker Boulevard / North 12th Street.

If you plan to visit the Gateway Arch—only a few minutes away—your heads-up will be Lucas Avenue. Take the next turn eastward onto Washington Avenue and continue toward the river. Just short of I-70, turn southward on Memorial Drive. Turn eastward again on Chestnut Street and you're there. Splendid, isn't it?

Make an easy return to the route via Market Street, a block south of Chestnut, and turn southward again on Tucker Boulevard. Continue on South Tucker—beyond a bend and passing beneath I-64 / US 40 and through an interchange that transitions into Gravois Avenue / SR 30. Continue through a bend at Grand Boulevard and bear west (away from the river) on Chippewa Street / SR 366.

Two blocks after crossing Hampton Avenue, Chippewa will bend to the southwest, and minutes later, Bancroft Avenue will be your heads-up for a double treat. At 6525 Chippewa stands the Donut Drive-In, with a renovated neon sign in the Route 66 tradition. And the donuts may be even better! This place gets raves from locals and travelers alike. The fare is mighty tasty, with some so light they seem ready to float away. Ted Drewes' Frozen Custard, another 66 stalwart, has been sold, but you can still find it a little farther along Chippewa.

Somewhere around Lansdowne Avenue, you'll also notice that Chippewa has magically changed its name to Watson Road. That means you're out of the city. Continue some 6 miles on Watson Road until you reach an opportunity to merge onto I-44 westbound, then take a deep breath. St. Louis is a magnificent city, but like most river towns, its layout can get you a little crazy. Still, you've done it and are now headed west into Ozark country.

Refer back to the Staunton-to-Sullivan map on page 17 to get your bearings, because you won't want to miss **Route 66 State Park**, the first of its kind. Missouri took the lead by announcing the first major park dedicated to the highway. This 409-acre recreational facility is on the site of Times Beach, an unfortunate community that was evacuated and leveled as part of a $200 million toxic cleanup. A Route 66 history exhibit and gift shop complement picnic areas, with hiking/biking trails and river access. It's a nice breather and a great stop on your tour. Use Exit 266.

If you are a neon fan or an admirer of renovated Route 66 motels, take Exit 261 and cross under I-44 to **Pacific**. There old Route 66 will lead you to the Sunset Motel, dating from 1946, with a stunning neon sign relit in 2009 after being dark for many years. The motel is being restored as well.

From Pacific, continue west on Business Loop 44 / Osage Street onto SR 100. As SR 100 heads west, go straight into SR AT. At the end of SR AT, cross US 50 where old Route 66 continues west as North Outer Road to County AH, crossing I-44 to the south side. Continue on South Outer Road and SR 47. At St. Clair, recross I-44 to the north side on SR 30 and continue on SR WW until it heads north, then continue on North Outer Road to— are you ready yet?—**Stanton**. Home of . . . ? That's right, the world-famous Meramec Caverns and alleged hideout of rascally Jesse James and his gang.

One of the most famous places along the old highway, Meramec Caverns was opened for the tourist trade in 1935 by champion roadside entrepreneur Lester Dill. Some locals still say that if Dill had not discovered the caverns, he'd have dug them himself. That's a fair assessment, because Lester B. Dill probably did invent that great American institution—the bumper sticker. So do make time for this attraction. Much of the copy recited by the tour guides hasn't changed since the 1930s. And if you don't happen to know who Kate Smith was, this is as good a place as any to find out.

Crossing to the south side at Stanton, and at the junction of SR JJ and SR W, continue west on South Outer Road. Through **Sullivan**, continue on the south side through **Bourbon**, where the main street is Old Highway 66. Actually, the name Bourbon is something of a misnomer since this is wine country.

If you missed Meramec Caverns or are a closet spelunker, Onondaga Cave, another old Route 66 attraction, just south of **Leasburg**, hasn't changed a bit. But renovation and upgrading have taken hold in **Cuba**. The 1934

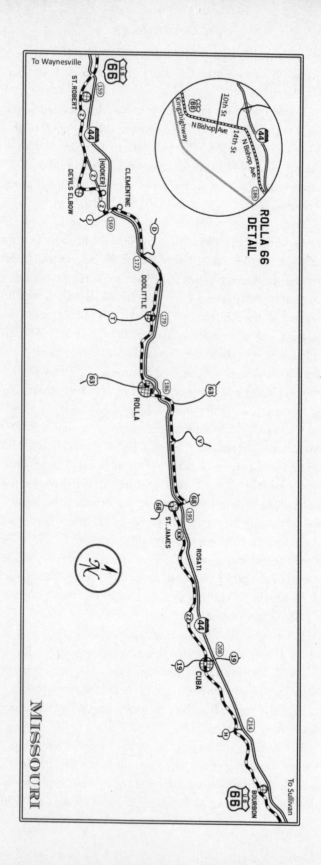

Wagon Wheel Motel at 901 East Washington Boulevard has undergone extraordinary renovation, from all-new wiring inside to removal of the vinyl siding and restoration of the original exterior. It's now vintage Americana, with a smile. All it lacks is a mirrored globe on a pedestal for the elves out front. By now it may even have one of those. Well recommended for an overnight. And just four miles west of Cuba, at the Outpost General Store, the giant rocking chair that attracts so many photographers during daylight hours now lights up the night as well.

From Cuba, continue on SR ZZ and KK into **St. James**. This area, **Rosati** especially, is known for its table grapes. If that strikes an appetite chord, plan to stop at one of the little grape stands along old Route 66. Only a few of the older stands remain, and there was a move afoot by the Missouri Department of Transportation to close down even the last of these tiny stands. It seems that people still like to stop, and now that the interstate makes it so difficult to get to the old road, folks just pull to the side of I-44 and visit the stands on foot. Yes, sir, sure does sound like it was the grape stands' fault, doesn't it? Some stands have moved to an access road. Otherwise, it would have been a complete standoff.

Just beyond St. James, there is a break in the old route, so rejoin I-44 or cross to the north side via SR 8 and 68 and continue to **Rolla**. Through town, the easier route to follow is Business Loop 44, which was a late alignment of old Route 66. Leaving town, follow Martin Spring Drive, which doubles as the south-side service road, and watch for the Totem Pole Trading Post—selling most anything from fuel and beer to fireworks since 1933. For most westbound travelers, this is the first taste of western-style advertising and its enticements.

Continue on to **Doolittle**, the town named for former air-race winner Jimmy Doolittle, who once bolstered sagging morale in the United States by coaxing a flight of sixteen standard-issue army B-25 bombers off the pitching deck of the U.S.S. *Hornet* for a raid on Tokyo, just a few months after the attack on Pearl Harbor. It wasn't a mighty blow; but it was a good sharp thumb in the eye at a time when not much was going right for us. As you drive down Doolittle's main street today, say a word of thanks that guys like Jimmy are around when they're needed.

Leaving town, you'll have to take I-44 for a short distance to SR D. For a real old-road treat, however, cross I-44, exiting at SR J southbound and turn west on SR Z to a place—one remaining structure and a cemetery is about the sum of it—called **Hooker**. The name brings a smile, but do you know the story of the word? Well, back during the Civil War, morale was as much a problem as supplies and ammunition. General Joseph Hooker, a self-distinguished Union general much given to the bottle, is said to have had a reserve of ladies wherever he campaigned. But the name *hooker* is more likely to have been given to the large number of professionals who traveled with wives and other camp followers. Some dispute this and other such stories, but the tale of a general who maintained morale by whatever means necessary persists. And the term is guaranteed to keep the place in the public eye, even if the town itself has faded into obscurity.

Whether you spot the site of Hooker or not, turn south at the first opportunity before Big Piney River. You're now right in the crook of **Devils Elbow**, a section of highway famous among Route 66 roadies for its river-bluff scenery and a lovely old steel-truss bridge built in 1923. There's no traffic on this loop, so take time for a stroll and perhaps a picnic lunch. Check locally on bridge conditions, though, before driving this section.

Continue west to return to the SR Z four-lane and roll on toward **St. Robert**. Cross to the north at the junction with Business Loop 44 and continue into **Waynesville**, where some interesting Romanesque architecture has been all but obscured by big-box stores.

Waynesville to Joplin

From Waynesville, follow SR 17 south across the interstate and through **Laquey**. Where SR 17 heads south, follow SR AB west into **Hazelgreen**. Continue on the south side of I-44, cross to the north side at SR F, and follow the north frontage road into **Lebanon**. The famous Munger Moss Motel is here, a Route 66 tradition exhibiting great

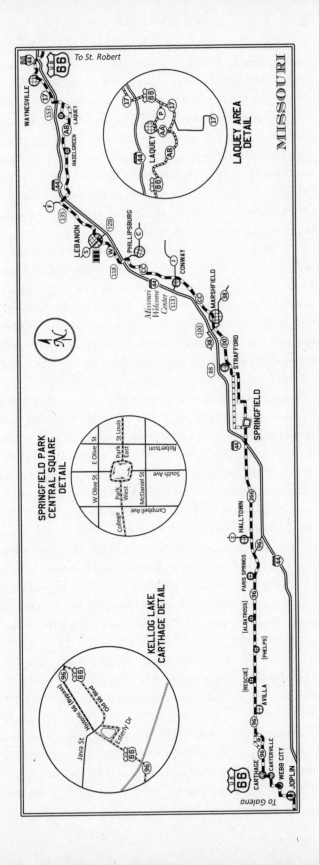

hospitality. Yet this modest roadside celebrity is more than a legend; it keeps pace with and is often on the forefront of the renaissance of Route 66. A completely restored neon sign, one of the most famous on the route, now graces the property. And Munger Moss's evolution over time mirrors the nature of travel in this country: separate cabins at first, carports in between later on, and what we recognize as a motel today as the last stage. Munger Moss has seen and helped pioneer them all. Rooms are even decorated to reflect many of the contributors to the Route 66 revival we now enjoy.

Yet there is more to this unassuming roadside community. At 915 South Jefferson Avenue, south of old Route 66 on SR 5 / 32, is the Lebanon-Laclede County Library, with an outstanding collection of publications reflecting the creation and development of Route 66 from its earliest days, now archived and available to writers and researchers worldwide—plus a fine Route 66 museum—all under one roof.

Departing Lebanon and joining SR W, you will find a fairly long run that gets well away from the interstate almost all the way into Springfield—and it's a beautiful drive through unspoiled farmland and small communities. At **Phillipsburg**, cross I-44 to the south and follow SR CC to **Conway**. There, flanking the interstate is the Missouri Welcome Center, with separate displays for westbound and eastbound travelers. One portrays Route 66 and landmarks across Missouri, while the other presents a history of the highway from border to border. What's more, the displays are regularly swapped. The welcome center also offers clever touches like sidewalks resembling a road surface and a collection of signage from the golden era of Route 66. In all, it's a great stop.

From Conway, continue on the south side through **Marshfield**. From **Strafford**, next, continue on SR OO into SR 744, which becomes Kearney Street in Springfield.

Springfield, Queen City of the Ozarks, is worth a browse, especially if you're doing a little photography or are interested in period architecture. From Kearney, turn south on Glenstone Avenue, then west onto St. Louis and

College Streets. After a few blocks, you'll notice the Shrine Mosque, a local curiosity and an old Route 66 landmark—built in 1923 and placed on the National Register of Historic Places in 1982. If you can imagine the former Grand Ole Opry in Nashville as it might have been designed by an itinerant Arab architect, you'll have a pretty good image of the mosque. It's wonderful, and still hosts some of the biggest acts around.

Farther west, you'll also pass the old calaboose on Central Square, near where Wild Bill Hickok killed Dave Tutt in one of those provoked shoot-outs for which the American West is infamous. As this story goes, Hickok had lost heavily to Tutt in a poker game. To buy time (literally), Hickok had given his pocket watch to Tutt to hold, with the express understanding that the watch would not be seen in public. Too embarrassing to Hickok, you see. But Tutt wore it anyway. Hickok killed him outright—there are plaques in the square to mark where each stood—and everyone settled down to watch Hickok's trial. The verdict was self-defense. But no one seemed to notice that, with Tutt now dead, Hickok had his watch back and no longer owed anything on his gambling debt.

But before we leave Springfield, something most important to Route 66 deserves mention, for this is the official birthplace of the highway and its famous double-sixes. On April 30, 1926, after long periods of haggling and inaction, officials favoring an entirely new highway were able to outwit proponents of an expanded Route 60 and a telegram went out. The new Chicago–Los

Angeles road would not be numbered 60 or 62. It would be Route 66.

The section of old Route 66 from Springfield west is a real treat. From the end of College Street, continue west on West Chestnut Expressway / Business Loop 44, and cross I-44. Continue west into SR 266 toward **Halltown**, often an interesting stop for antiquers. Go west through **Paris Springs Junction** for a cruise on old, old Route 66, rather than jogging south onto SR 96. At the junction with SR N, cross to the south of SR N. Turn west from SR N at the first intersection and cross the old steel-truss bridge. Continue through Casey's Corner at what was once Spencer, cross to the north of SR 96 at the stop, and continue toward Carthage.

Town names along this stretch of Route 66 sing a special song in passing: **Albatross**, **Phelps**, **Rescue** . . . **Log City**, and **Stone City** are only shadows of what they were. Indeed, from this section of the old route on west, through parts of Oklahoma, Texas, New Mexico, and Arizona, the number of abandoned businesses and highway attractions increases greatly. In some ways, that's a sad fact.

But there is a more cheerful view, championed by observers like John Brinkerhoff Jackson, that there is a great need for relics like these. Since we can experience history only through our imaginations, they suggest, the ruins we encounter serve as props for any journey of the mind in time. In viewing some roadside ruin, then, we are better able to re-create for ourselves the period in which it stood. An interesting thought—that by seeing clearly what remains, each of us gives some ruin a second life. A chance to exist again, as it once was, as a projection of our mind's eye.

Just knowing this can make the traveling more passionate, the seeing more profound, as you make your way along this old road—which is itself a relic. Yet a relic that you may revive, if only for a moment, by your passing.

Less than a mile after **Avilla**, beyond the Victory Baptist Church, jog left, then right again along a line of old telephone poles. At the Y stop sign, jog right, then left onto SR 96.

Carthage is next, and it too is special. A businesslike

county seat, it is peopled with individualists of the first water—the notorious Belle Starr was born here. There is also a strong creative thread in Carthage that seems to go way back. Still following SR 96, take at least a moment for the town square and the classic Jasper County Courthouse. The clock has been reinstalled after taking the cure for striking thirteen too often. And the courthouse lawn looks pretty good, too.

Remember the Missouri sense of humor? Carthage does. Some years back, when the lawn was redone, someone slipped turnip seed into the replanting mixture. The grass was only mediocre, but embarrassed officials had a bumper turnip crop.

Entering Carthage on Central Avenue, you'll have a choice. If you're a B&B fan, turn south on Garrison Avenue / SR 571 and east on Centennial Avenue, go three blocks to Grand Avenue, and turn south again. At 1615 is the Grand Avenue Bed and Breakfast, a lovingly restored Queen Anne Victorian home, now listed on the National Register. It's charming and even comes with an occasional ghost. Once a cigar-smoking antifeminist, the friendly apparition has apparently seen the error of his ways and now contents himself with fixing popcorn in the microwave at odd hours. Definitely worth an overnight.

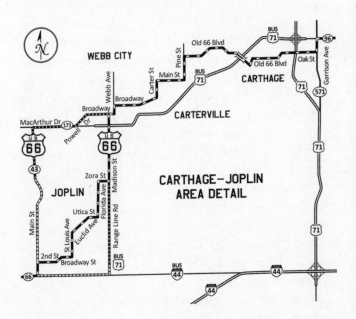

To continue through Carthage from Central, turn left on Garrison Avenue and right on Oak Street. Cross US 71, then bear left on Old 66 Boulevard and turn left at the stop. Continue to the T, turning left on Pine, then right onto Main Street in Carterville. Follow Main through the S-curve onto Carter Street and enter **Webb City**, following Broadway to Madison Street. Then turn left and continue on Business US 71 toward **Joplin**.

Peaceful **Joplin** sits atop countless abandoned mining tunnels and a rough history—beginning with a two-town rivalry. A local judge and his friend, a Methodist minister named Joplin, had established a nice lead-rich town when a competing town called Murphysburg sprang up just across Turkey Creek.

The judge got himself all riled up about that, and the other town's developer, Murphy, got counterriled. Soon someone brought in a bushwhacker called Three-Fingered Pete. Then someone else hired a brawler called Reckless Bill, and everybody began having at it on a regular basis. Mining got all mixed up with religion, which got all mixed up with the law and the egos of those in both towns. In the end, it became such an awful mess that the state legislature stepped in, Siamesed the two towns under the single name City of Joplin, and told everyone to behave themselves or they wouldn't get a railroad.

So things settled down quickly and the miners returned to their labors all along this old section of the route. In fact they worked so hard and long that the road itself developed a habit of falling into abandoned tunnels. Several detours have been necessary since a cave-in along the road back in 1939. As this is being written, there are no new detours near Galena or down the highway. Still, drive lightly—and when you walk, don't stamp your feet. You might fall right on through.

The easier way through Joplin follows Business US 71 to SR 66 west, but the more interesting route follows the zigzag shown on the map. Near the border you may notice a few last-chance saloons that recall the time when Kansas was dry. These are no places to go now, though, so save your two-step for Texas.

West of Joplin, keep watch for Old 66 Boulevard. The newer SR 66 alignment to the southwest continues on to

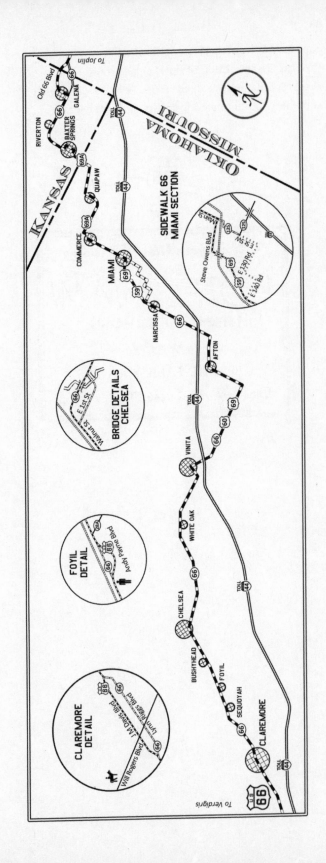

Kansas, but a northerly bend here will put you on another rare surviving section of the original route. There's a nice resurrected feeling about these few miles, which have somehow found protection through local use.

KANSAS

There are only a dozen or so miles of old Route 66 in Kansas. But they are part of a saw-toothed run from Joplin, Missouri, to Vinita, Oklahoma, that's a crackerjack stretch of highway and history. If you've ever wondered why all the old road dogs seem to have huge nautical compasses mounted in their cars or camper cabs, one look at the map for this part of old Route 66 will provide the answer. When you're on a road that zigzags along section lines rather than following a more direct course, it's easy to guess your direction only when it's early or late in the day. The rest of the time you'd better have some other means of knowing which way you're headed. Kansas doesn't make it difficult, but it isn't easy either.

All of which fits with the old Middle American tradition of never admitting that you don't know something. Most people who grew up anywhere from Ohio to Oklahoma know not to ask directions of strangers or service station attendants. Instead of saying that they don't know (when they don't), well-intentioned midwesterners will just give you the most plausible answer they can think of. And it seldom has anything to do with accuracy.

There are a couple of other things to remember as you roll from southern Missouri on into Kansas and Oklahoma. The first is that this area is pretty close to the buckle on the Bible Belt, so you'd best save any snappy ecumenical jokes you have for later. The other thing is to think twice before ordering Italian in these parts. Oklahomans, for example, take their religion and the way their meat is cooked pretty seriously. There are more churches and barbecue joints between the Kansas border and Oklahoma City than many people see in a lifetime. On other matters—with the thundering exception of football—Oklahomans are far more laid-back.

It's a little different just the other side of the line. In Kansas, they tend to take everything seriously. It's not a place to cut up much. Especially in a restaurant at Sunday brunch. Some of this traces back to the kind of righteous single-mindedness with which issues have been settled here. People who got caught in the cross fire between Quantrill's Raiders and the Jayhawkers, during the Civil War period, quickly learned that most everything about life could get serious in a hurry. Later, as the labor movement was beginning in the zinc and lead mines of this region, both the company goons and militant union members took the matter right into the streets. There were times during the mid-1930s when old Route 66 itself ran red, usually with the blood of determined strikers. This is country that has been cleared, farmed, and mined the hard way. And parents have taught their children well.

But a hundred years of conflict in this little corner of Kansas has produced something of great value to the traveler. The people here along the old road are as clear and honest and forthcoming as can be found anywhere. What's more, they have a sense of history and a knowledge of themselves that sets them apart.

No one dawdles much here. Work still comes before much else. Of all the states through which old Route 66 passed, Kansas was among the first to see that the highway was properly paved in concrete. The towns here—Galena,

Riverton, Baxter Springs—are also among the quietest and most serene you'll find. Take a stroll down by one of the rivers. Walk along a neighborhood street. Listen to the crickets and the banging of the screen doors. There are only a few miles of Kansas on the old route, but this place is a big part of the true America we all carry somewhere in our hearts.

It's no wonder Dorothy and Toto were so happy to be home again.

Galena to Baxter Springs

Continuing on the older alignment through **Galena**, turn south on Main Street. Long before Prohibition, when the mining boom could still be heard, this was called Red Hot Street in Galena. And it was that, no doubt about it. The saloons and bawdy houses stayed open twenty-four hours a day, keeping the miners picked clean from payday to payday.

In the beginning, the town of Empire had richer mines than Galena. So, to prevent unwelcome Galenans from making a daily beeline for the better diggings, the protective folks of Empire built a high fence of timbers along the town's border. Galena waited some months until the entire fence was completed, then simply burned it to the ground—so much for the fortress concept. Later, when the mines in Empire began to play out, Galena annexed the town. Departing Galena-Empire, continue on SR 66.

In **Riverton**, about four blocks after crossing the Spring River, watch for Eisler Brothers' General Store to your right, located on the route since 1925. Nice helpful folks. After that get ready for your zigzag driving adventure as the old road makes a dozen ninety-degree turns across Kansas and eastern Oklahoma.

West of Riverton, at the end of SR 66 and the US 69A / 400 junction, continue west onto Beasley Road and bend left onto 50th Street. Watch for one of the last remaining rainbow-style concrete-truss bridges, Brush Creek Arch Bridge. Names don't exactly go up in lights around here, but this span was for years a marquee for locally sown wild oats. Continued existence of the bridge was threatened with demolition, but the Kansas Route 66 Association made a great save and you can still drive over it. Or if you're ready to make good on your promises, you might reserve this charming setting for a wedding. Either way, follow 50th as it becomes Willow Avenue, and bend left onto 3rd Street. At US 69A / Military Avenue, turn toward **Baxter Springs**. There, at 1101 Military Avenue, you'll find the charming Cafe on the Route, housed in the 1876 Baxter Bank Building along with the Little Brick Inn B&B. Both have been recommended. But don't let the locals jaw you too much about the great Jesse James bank heist of 1876. Historians say it didn't happen. The notorious robber was up to no good, all right, but he was up to it somewhere else.

On U.S. 66 and 77

2 blocks north of State Capitol

PARK-O-TELL

OKLAHOMA CITY, OKLAHOMA

100 modern fireproof rooms

Free Garage » Excellent Coffee Shop

OKLAHOMA

When you talk about outlaws in Oklahoma, it's important to distinguish between regular outlaws and elected
outlaws. The state has certainly had more than its share of
both. First came all the sodbusters who jumped the line
early during the great land rush. They undoubtedly set the
trend for everybody. Later, when some political hustlers
decided that Oklahoma City would make a more profitable
center for state government, they simply stole the Great
Seal from the existing state capitol in Guthrie and hauled
it on down to its present site. One result is that good out-
lawing became something of a fifth estate in Oklahoma.

Like many of the better class of outlaws, Jesse James and
his pals started out in Missouri but spent a lot of time in
these parts. So did Pretty Boy Floyd, an Oklahoman from
age five, who soon became a Robin Hood of the 1930s. An
expert in the bank-robbing business, Pretty Boy always
found time to tear up whatever farm mortgages he could

find around a bank. And when on the lam, he is said to have paid poor farm families for a meal—and their silence, of course—with a $1,000 bill tucked under his napkin.

All across the state, Depression-ridden people understood his motives and were cheered by his exploits. So they defended Pretty Boy and cared for him as their own. When the hapless Floyd was finally gunned down by the FBI, twenty thousand mourners turned out for his burial. It was the biggest funeral Oklahoma has ever seen. As for Ma Barker and her sons, together with Bonnie Parker, Clyde Barrow, Machine Gun Kelly, and the rest of the outlaws turned killers, good riddance. No folk songs are sung about them. None need be.

For many Route 66 travelers, Oklahoma has often been no more than a place to be driven through quickly in order to get to the good stuff farther west. Too bad for them. Because Oklahoma, once truly seen and fully experienced, is one of the most beautiful and openhanded places to be found anywhere. Cyclists and hikers could do no better than pedal or hoof their way through the gently rolling country from the Kansas border to Oklahoma City.

In the western reaches of the state, the land is even more beautiful, lying rumpled in all directions like a giant designer bedsheet, small farms and friendly towns among the creases. More attractive to automobile drivers or motorcyclists than to bicycle riders, perhaps, but magnificent nonetheless.

For real pit-barbecue freaks, however, the entire state is a groaning board. Closet cases of smoke fever may be forced out into the open, and all but the most devout vegetarians will be sorely tested. So you may as well learn the tune: "Get your ribs on Route 66."

The remarkable thing is that in Oklahoma as nowhere else, art and architecture go hand in hand with history, down-home hospitality, and the sweetness of the green-on-red land. Truly the soul of old Route 66, Oklahoma is well worth knowing. Take some time here. Let the people of Oklahoma get to know you, too.

Nearly all of old Route 66 has been preserved and remains in daily use throughout eastern Oklahoma. Since the interstate turnpike is a toll road here, most local and regional travel is done on the Free Road—old Route 66. And an excellent highway it is, too. You'll have little difficulty following this unbroken 260-mile section of the old road as it meanders along from the Kansas border to Oklahoma City.

Quapaw to Tulsa

From Baxter Springs, follow US 69A south into **Quapaw**. If it's coming on nighttime, you may be able to do a little ghost-busting here. One and a half miles east of Quapaw, on a bluff called Devil's Promenade near the Spring River, is the home of Spooklight, an apparition that once drew as many as a thousand cars per night during the peak spook season. Spooklight (no joke here) appears as a dancing, bobbing, rolling ball of light, seen in these parts regularly for years. Sometimes Spooklight has even been seen entering parked cars. Also no joke is that some unsavory types are attracted to the area. Be sure to check locally before going out there.

There are lots of theories, but thus far nothing approaching an adequate explanation. Scientists and army technicians of nearly every stripe have tested this and that, but to no avail. One of the better technical theories holds that Spooklight is really only a wandering atmospheric refraction of headlights on the nearby highway. But that falls a little short when it is noted that Spooklight was first seen by the Quapaw Indians in the mid-1800s. Not exactly a lot of cars around back then. Undaunted by the lack of a theoretical structure, Spookie just keeps on hanging out here—to nearly everyone's delight.

Unless you're spooked, follow US 69A south, then west from Quapaw and jog through **Commerce**, home of Mickey (the Commerce Comet) Mantle. Entering town southbound, jog west on Commerce and south again on Main Street, heading on down to **Miami** (pronounced My-am-uh).

Continue through Miami on Main Street, and if possible, take time for a look at the ornate Mission Revival–style Coleman Theater, built at the onset of the Great Depression and still surviving. And as the result of years of restoration and community support, it's a beauty.

At Steve Owens Boulevard, turn west to follow a newer alignment of Route 66, or continue south on SR 125 to drive—with care—over an older nine-foot-wide section, sometimes called Sidewalk 66. There are two sections of this roadbed; this appears to be the less fragile of the two. Still, it *cannot* handle heavy-duty trucks or motor homes. From the Steve Owens intersection, continue south on E Street SW through the jog. Turn west again on East 130 Road, jog south for a bit, then west on East 140 Road to junction with US 59 / 69 / SR 66 southbound. See the Galena–Claremore map on page 35 for details.

From Miami, follow US 69 through **Narcissa**, join US 60, then cross under the turnpike and continue to Afton. Because so much tourist business has been lost to through traffic on the interstate, most attractions in this area have an uncertain existence; they come and they go.

But in **Afton**, you may be in luck. David and Laurel Kane have restored Afton Station from top to bottom and stuffed it with vintage Packard automobiles. That's right, Packards! Perhaps the greatest line of cars to be squeezed out by the Big Three after World War II. Other memorabilia and an astonishing postcard collection fill the place as well, but it's the old Sunray D-X station and a showroom of Packards that can leave you a little short of breath. Roadies everywhere wish the Kanes good fortune and trust they'll be around when you visit.

From Afton, continue south, then west on US 60 / 69 and SR 60. **Vinita** is next, named for Vinnie Ream, the sculptress whose rendering of Abraham Lincoln now graces the nation's capital. Through Vinita, follow SR 66 US 60 / 69 / East Illinois Avenue through a turn south onto South Wilson Street. Bend west and continue on to **White Oak**. Then continue southwest on the Free Road into **Chelsea**, the very first oil-patch town and one of the few to have a perfectly preserved example of a 1913 Sears mail-order house located a block northwest of 66 at West 10th and Olive Streets. Imagine near-perfect craftsmanship arriving in a box, ready for assembly. This is a private residence, however, so take care not to disturb if you park nearby for a look.

Farther south, the village of **Bushyhead** is all but gone now. But **Foyil** has a showpiece or two. A few miles east of town on SR 28A is Galloway's Totem Pole Park, where you can see the results of that flash of artistic genius some roadside entrepreneurs find in themselves. Make sure your camera has plenty of juice, though. The place is a challenge to portray. Foyil also boasts a nice loop of old, old Route 66—in its original pink concrete—curving through town.

Toward the west end of town is an aging monument to Andy Payne, the slight twenty-year-old Oklahoma contender in the 1928 Bunion Derby footrace from Los Angeles to New York. He covered the 3,400-mile distance—his running time was just over 573 hours—to finish first in one of the most mismanaged events in the history of organized running. Oklahomans remained confident of his winning, in the face of derision, because they knew something that bettors from the outside did not know or believe: Andy Payne was in the habit of racing against a horse on his way to school in Foyil.

On down the road, **Claremore** is worth some extra time for a visit to the Will Rogers Memorial. Claremore is also the hometown of Lynn Riggs, author of *Green Grow the Lilacs*, on which the 1944 Pulitzer Prize–winning musical *Oklahoma!* is based. Entering town, angle west at the first signal and continue parallel to SR 66 on J. M. Davis Boulevard. This is the old route and motel row in Claremore. The Claremore Motor Inn, though not a landmark, is comfortable and a good place to stay. Also, keep a nose-scan going for Pits Barbeque. It's on the left and one of the better barbecue places around.

Farther along, both Davis and Riggs Boulevards intersect with Will Rogers Boulevard. Turn northwest and watch for Will Rogers Memorial signage on the right. The place is remarkable, a grand reminder of what it meant to have Will among us for a time. He knew that life couldn't be made easier, though it could be made better. He offered everyone that secret—with a smile to start things off.

Return to SR 66 and continue southwest on the Free

Road. After the highway bends west, watch for the non-identical twin spans over the Verdigris River / Bird Creek. Many feel compelled to capture an image of this odd couple of bridges—some even call them Felix and Oscar—and a few travelers are bothered by the difference. But these grand through-truss bridges might not be noticed at all if they matched.

Cresting the next hill, watch for the old Blue Whale Amusement Park on the north side nearing **Catoosa**. It may only be a photo opportunity now, but who knows? Catoosa has grit, as well as a name referring to People of the Light. It's not clear, though, if the Cherokee were seeing the same kind of light as the Quapaw.

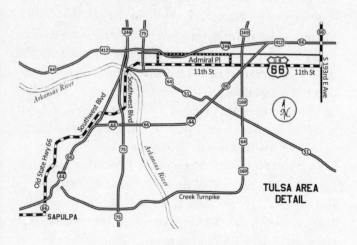

TULSA AREA
DETAIL

Tulsa to Oklahoma City

Nearing **Tulsa**, the Free Road can be crowded, so keep a sharp eye out for the SR 167 junction. Tulsa is one of the most fascinating cities on Route 66, so plan on taking the route through town rather than I-44 / SR 66, where virtually nothing of interest is visible.

In fact, take special care *not* to follow SR 66 up onto the interstate. Instead, continue straight south on 193rd Avenue (SR 167) past Admiral Place, and turn west again on 11th Street, where you'll find great architecture by day and fine neon by night. A section of Admiral Place is shown as an optional alignment between Mingo Road and

Lewis Avenue. But the action in renovation and continuing redevelopment—Art Deco, restored neon, streetscapes, and a host of Route 66 attractions—is on 11th Street.

Arched gateways will welcome westbound travelers to Tulsa at 11707 East 11th Street, while eastbound travelers will find an identical span at 4339 Southwest Boulevard. And if you arrive during evening hours, you won't miss the lighted Route 66 shields.

At the intersection of East 11th Street and Mingo Road is Tulsa's Route 66 Mingo Greenway—a mile-long park on the 1926–32 alignment, with walking trails, interpretive information, and picnic tables. A renovated 1950s motor court, the Desert Hills Hotel, comes up at 5520 East 11th Street, with a classic neon sign.

Cultural Crossroads, on 11th Street at Yale, is a fine urban surprise. Engaging all four corners in this 1920s Tudor Revival neighborhood, and listed on the National Register of Historic Places, you'll find heritage murals, Tally's Route 66 Café, and a Route 66 deli. Eclectic? You bet.

Rossi Brothers' renovated gas station, echoing the 1930s, is at 3509 East 11th Street, and is also listed on the National Register. The theme is very clear along 11th Street: Route 66 and period architecture. Skelly Field, visible on the University of Tulsa campus, helps carry the ball for Art Deco. And the 1920s Casa Loma Hotel (Campbell Building) at 2626–2648 East 11th Street, renovated as shops and living space, may now be on the National Register as well. This is a splendid Neo-Spanish Colonial Revival building, with twin towers and rare details.

The iconic 20-by-40-foot Meadow Gold neon sign at 1324 East 11th Street visually anchors a Plains Commercial–style pavilion and offers a remarkable display at dusk, as it outshines city lights. And the real prize is yet to come. At 401 East 11th Street is the 1929 Warehouse Market. The tower will draw you to toward the colorful terra cotta trim. Long neglected, this marvelous Art Deco structure is being renewed, showing signs of again becoming the neighborhood centerpiece it once was, and an anchor for local redevelopment.

Peoria Avenue is your heads-up for bends and turns in the route through western Tulsa. At South Elgin Avenue,

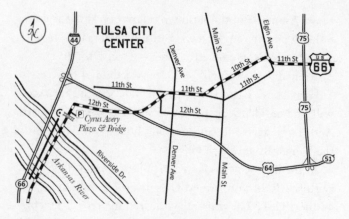

bend north and then west again on East 10th Street, which will merge again into West 11th Street. A half block beyond South Denver Avenue, West 11th bends southwest again for an expressway overcrossing and becomes West 12th Street—and for the record, I've no idea how this got so confusing. Do you suppose that expressway sprawl has something to do with it?

In either event, turn south at Southwest Boulevard and your efforts will be rewarded. As a pedestrian skywalk comes into view toward the river, turn into the parking area for the Cyrus Avery Plaza. It's a grand place to stretch a bit (or let the little ones get loopy for a while), see the old 11th Street Bridge, and learn a little of Cyrus Avery, the Oklahoma promoter who fostered the original concept of Route 66. A highway-size bronze, *East Meets West*, commemorates the man, his family, and our Route 66 legacy.

First, the bridge: an open-spandrel arch design built in 1916, which carried traffic for over sixty years and survived threats of demolition for another twenty until its deck could be stabilized. Cyrus Avery's story is more complex, as was the man himself. Unlike many promoters, Avery understood the principle of doing well by doing good. That's an important distinction. He sometimes tinkered with the route to favor business interests. Yet it was Avery who pushed, prodded, and sweet-talked an apathetic bureaucracy into approving the first all-weather highway from Chicago to the West Coast . . . via Tulsa, and a bridge spanning the Arkansas River that would carry the load.

From Avery Plaza, cross the river on Southwest Boulevard / SR 66 and continue south along the eastern side of

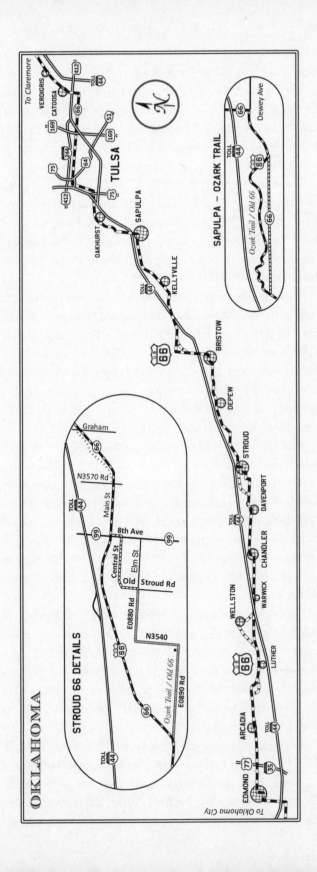

OKLAHOMA

To Claremore
VERDIGRIS
CATOOSA
TOLL 44
412
169
51
169
244
64
75
TULSA
412
75
SAPULPA
OAKHURST
KELLYVILLE
TOLL 44

SAPULPA – OZARK TRAIL

66
Dewey Ave
TOLL 44
66
Ozark Trail / Old 66
66

US 66

BRISTOW
DEPEW
STROUD
DAVENPORT
TOLL 44
CHANDLER
WARWICK
WELLSTON
LUTHER
US 66
ARCADIA
TOLL 44
EDMOND
77
35
To Oklahoma City

STROUD 66 DETAILS

Graham
66
N3570 Rd
TOLL 44
Main St
99
8th Ave
99
Central St
Elm St
Old Stroud Rd
E0880 Rd
N3540
Ozark Trail / Old 66
E0890 Rd
66
66
TOLL 44

I-244. A new expression of interest in the Red Fork area, combining the old highway with regional history, comes in the form of Route 66 Transportation Village / Route 66 Station. A 154-foot oil derrick replica has been built to attract the eye from a distance, and on site you'll find a 1941 Frisco 4500 steam locomotive, a Pullman car, a caboose, and in time a full range of interpretive displays.

Further reflecting the railroad tradition is Ollie's Station Restaurant at 4070 Southwest Boulevard. Here you'll find not only a rail-history theme, but railroad-style entrées, and—are you ready?—miniature trains running overhead around the dining area. If you're a train buff or a model railroader, this is the place.

Close by, at West 41st Street, you'll cross to the west side of the interstate. Near **Oakhurst**, Southwest Boulevard continues as Old Sapulpa Road / Frankoma Road / Old State Highway, swinging wide of the I-44 corridor. You'll then cross under I-44 and junction with SR 66 to continue south into **Sapulpa**. Continue south, with a heads-up at Hobson Avenue, for a turn west with SR 66 onto East Dewey Avenue.

Sapulpa has learned to use art cosmetically. Empty store windows often become display cases for photographic prints. Boarded-up windows in the side of a two-story building are transformed into a hand-painted triptych. And if you're getting hungry, Norma's Cafe—reopened as Diamond Bart's Café after Norma passed on—has been serving roadies for years at 408 North Mission Street, on the corner of the intersection leading west through town on SR 66.

Departing Sapulpa, watch for Rock Creek Bridge, an old steel-truss bridge off to the northwest, about a mile west of town. It's just beyond an intersection marked, curiously enough, Highway 66 and Old Highway 66—perhaps the only acknowledgment of both alignments anywhere in the country. The bridge is especially photogenic with its well-preserved redbrick deck.

Continue through an S-curve to a junction with the Ozark Trail and Old 66. This is a charming bit of the old highway that has seen little change over the years. Rejoin SR 66 / SR 33 heading for **Kellyville**, **Bristow**, and **Depew**, which interweave a number of abandoned sections of old, old Route 66 on the northwest side of the Free Road, some of which can be driven for short distances. Two very nice loops of older alignment begin about two miles beyond Kellyville. The first is just past the interstate overpass and rates a slow top-down drive.

Another angular section comes up a few miles farther on. An airfield—probably an airmail stop—was sited along the west leg of this loop and shows up on old maps. No one has spotted it yet, though. Maybe you'll be the first. So do some exploring and find your own favorite little tree-shaded country lane. Remember to keep an eye out for lines of weathered telephone poles and old cuts through the trees. On reaching the division point between SR 66 and West 181st Street, continue straight ahead for the old route rather than taking the newer cutoff. Turn south onto SR 48 to rejoin SR 66, which will cross under I-44 and continue through Bristow and Depew to **Stroud.**

Rolling into Stroud, you'll find an old—and impassable—section of Route 66 on the northwest side, beginning at Graham and ending at N3570 Road. Continue along Main Street to check out the Rock Café. For years it has been a twenty-four-hour must-stop for travelers through this area. And, except for its rock walls, the place burned to the ground in 2008. But like much of Route 66, it's back—even its steel grill survived—and serving up everything from veggie nachos to chicken-fried steak.

If the name Stroud sounds a little tough for this sleepy little town now, it's because the place once really was tough. Cattle drovers shipped from here, the nearby Indian Territory was dry, and a string of bars made lots of money selling hooch of questionable character to everybody. Now Stroud is the kind of place where, if you are doing a late wash, you lock up the Laundromat after yourself. Nice town.

For a drive down old, old 66 and a historic chunk of the Ozark Trail—but only in good weather—turn south on 8th Avenue, west on Central Street, south on Old Stroud Road, and west again on E0880 Road. This is the old unpaved roadbed, and it continues south on N3540 Road, past an Ozark Trail marker at the right-angle turn onto E0890 Road, to rejoin SR 66 westbound.

Approaching **Davenport**, continue straight at the 6th Street curve for the center of town. Otherwise, follow SR 66 as marked. Locals take some pride in their rolling streets here. Main is known as Snuff Street—"drive a block and take a dip." Beyond Davenport, the old route heads on into Chandler.

As you enter **Chandler** on First Street, the Lincoln Motel on the right was built in 1939 and is an example of cottage-style tourist courts—the word *motel* was created in 1925, but hadn't got around much—on or off the route. Angling south on Manvel, you can gas up at a vintage service station if you like. Midway through town, you'll notice the Lincoln County Museum, with its striking red stone exterior and an interesting Route 66 collection. There's also a fine old bakery and Granny's Country Kitchen, both on Manvel and recommended by locals.

Yet here's a bit of history you won't see. But it lives with us in almost all pop / rock music today. Every serious guitarist or anyone buying records back in the fifties, knows of Les Paul. Aside from his stratospheric playing, he invented the solid-body electric guitar, echo effects (by using a bathroom at first), and an ingenious method of multitracking now taken for granted. With wife Mary Ford, he also defined the term *hit*—they sold millions of every recording (when a thousand was considered terrific). And he was in crisis when he was doing it. In 1948, east of Chandler, Paul's car went down an embankment along Route 66. His right arm was shattered and amputation was recommended. Les would have none of it. He asked that the arm and elbow be permanently fused at an angle that would allow his shoulder to do the work. That accident on Route 66 changed Les Paul's life—and our music—forever.

Farther west, if you're driving something like a Mustang GT or a Corvette, there are some perfectly banked left and right sweepers through this section that can make you cry for more good old roads. Clearly this highway was designed by men who drove, not by men who budgeted. And it's not hard to tell the difference in the result, is it?

In **Arcadia**, you'll find a mix of old and new that typifies Highway 66—it's rooted in the past yet always changing. Much of the town has an early thirties feeling. And the famous 1898 Round Barn has been restored, due in no small part to Route 66 travelers who chipped in their dimes and dollars to help out the dedicated preservationists here. The exterior is fine now, and the timbered interior dome is mind-boggling.

Yet there's also a new kid on the block: POPS! With a towering 66-foot pop bottle, this place honors the highway's commercial, get-it-all-here past, yet soars into the future with stunning, unexpected architectural design. POPS offers a full spectrum of over 500 soda flavors, plus a shake shop and a restaurant serving breakfast, lunch, and dinner. And yep, you can even fill 'er up at the gas pumps out front. It takes confidence to plant a place like this along an old highway, but it always has. POPS: no better sign that the old highway is alive and well.

West of Arcadia, cross I-35 and head on into **Edmond** on SR 66 / US 77. Little of the old Route 66 feeling remains here. But Edmond is a university town and enjoys a lovely campus. Continue westbound on Second Street in Edmond—do not follow SR 66 onto I-44—and turn south on Broadway / US 77.

Oklahoma City to Texola

For a microtour of Route 66 remnants through **Oklahoma City**—plus some special highlights—follow Broadway Extension Highway south from Edmond and

take the Kelley Avenue exit. Continue south on Kelley and enter I-44 westbound, stay to the right, and exit at the next off-ramp for North Lincoln Avenue.

Heading south on the long-term Lincoln section of Route 66, you'll have a striking view of the Oklahoma state capitol—famous for the oil-producing rigs on its grounds—and its impressive dome. Circle the capitol and head west on Northwest 23rd Street.

For larger centers like Oklahoma City, through-town highways meant little compared to local commerce—the route was shuffled around with little regard to travelers. So what remains of Route 66-era businesses or attractions here is increasingly precious. And with some of the highest community volunteer rates in the country, the city is making it pay off along the Route 66 corridor.

A glowing example is the neon-lit Tower Theater marquee, now restored to full glory. The 1937 theater is an important anchor for the redevelopment going on in this district. And the city could do no better. Hats off to all the folks who stayed the course and are making this happen. You'll find the Tower Theater at 425 Northwest 23rd Street, on the north side near Walker Avenue, just minutes west of the Capitol.

From this point on—north and west—you'll have several choices, so it's a good idea to read ahead a bit. You may continue on the 23rd Street route and turn north on May Avenue to follow SR 66 west on the expressway. (Note: the expressway is not Historic Route 66, which was obliterated, though you can reconnect with the original roadway at North Overholser Drive, just beyond Bethany.)

That said, the recommended route for photos, food, and fun is to turn north onto North Classen Boulevard, six blocks past Walker Avenue, with an immediate heads-up for the giant Townley Dairy milk bottle—a classic in commercial architecture—on a triangle of land bounded by Northwest 24th Street and North Millay Avenue. The brick structure has since housed everything from delis to nail salons, yet the Townley bottle remains aloof—selling only itself regardless of what tenants are below. In early morning or late afternoon lighting it's one of the most striking images on Route 66.

For a special treat, continue a few minutes north on Classen Boulevard, passing under SR 66 to a smooth right bend: Classen Curve—shown as an asterisk on the map. It's a new look for the city. This sleek area with a small-town feeling offers the kind of downtown experience that once marked towns throughout the Midwest.

Even better, as any roadie knows, it's good fortune to find at least two reasons to stop anywhere. And the curve does not disappoint. Excellent restaurants are here, from full-on vegan at 105 Degrees to the European-style Cafe 501, and the wonderful something-for-everyone Republic Gastropub. Take a look at menus and prices to see what appeals most.

All of which reminds us that Route 66 is always evolving, though few if any, anticipated the sweep of the highway's renaissance. Yet—and this is important—Jeanette Koenig stepped up to name her shop *Route 66* before the revival ever began. Here, you'll find an eclectic collection served up with elegance. Items ranging from the useful to highway chic. Handcrafted, made-in-America items created from recycled road-borne components are a mainstay. Bicycle chains that once traveled the old highway, now re-created as clocks; purses made from auto license plates; embroidered Route 66 patches; and limited-edition Route 66 watches like no other. The selection is varied and you'll find Jeanette to be witty, warm, and especially welcoming to travelers in from the road. In an urban setting that in itself is special; be sure to let her know. . . .

So if you're looking for an exclusive item to take home from your tour of the highway, the Route 66 shop is a wonderful place to browse. To be sure of hours and location, check in by phone at 405-848-6166.

To rejoin Route 66, head back south to SR 66 west-bound and pass through **Bethany**. Jog south a mile after Council Road, cross the bridge and follow lake breezes along North Overholser Drive and Northwest 36th Street toward Yukon.

Back in 1941, this lake was the first and only body of water in Oklahoma to be officially designated as a seaplane base. Pan American Airways' graceful Clippers were all the rage and transcontinental seaplane travel was considered to be the next major development in air travel. But

by the time World War II had ended, military and civil-
ian engineers had built thousands of miles of long concrete runways almost everywhere. In many places, whole
neighborhoods were flattened to make way. Yet, the seaplane era was declared to be over, and Lake Overholser's
hopes faded with the times. Some now say it was a mis-
take. They may be right.

At the far side of the lake, bear right at the Y intersection and head west to Mustang Road. Jog north and take
the four-lane westbound to **Yukon**.

Many of the buildings on the main street here preserve
the feeling of Route 66 towns. Yukon also marks a transition from Midwest to West. From here on, as farms give
way to ranches, the drawls you hear will become more pronounced and the West we recognize from movies begins.
If you observe closely, you'll actually see the change taking
place between here and the Texas border.

Also, should you happen to be in Yukon at day's end,
check out the huge chase-light sign atop the Yukon Flour
Mill. It can be positively mesmerizing.

Approaching **El Reno** on the old highway, watch for
the Big 8 Motel, advertising itself as AMARILLO'S FINEST.
And no, the owners are not confused. The sign is a legacy
from the movie *Rain Man*, part of which was shot here. In
fact you can stay in the room—set-dressed just as it was
featured in the film. Just ask for Room 117. Now all you
need is a 1949 Buick with portholes. Or Dustin's phone
number.

Dynaflowing on west, continue straight, or for the older
alignment turn north on Sheppard Avenue at the signal,
then curve west along the cemetery on Elm Street. At the
water-tower signal, turn north on Choctaw Avenue / US 81.
Just a few blocks along, on the right side, is the remarkable
BPOE Lodge. This building was once part of an Oklahoma
territorial exhibit (remember, Oklahoma was not yet a
state) at the St. Louis Exposition of 1904—the fair that
introduced hot dogs and ice cream to the world. When
the exhibit closed, the building was disassembled and
brought to El Reno as a permanent structure. If the Elks
are not the Best People On Earth, as the acronymic name
of their lodge suggests, they are certainly among the most
industrious.

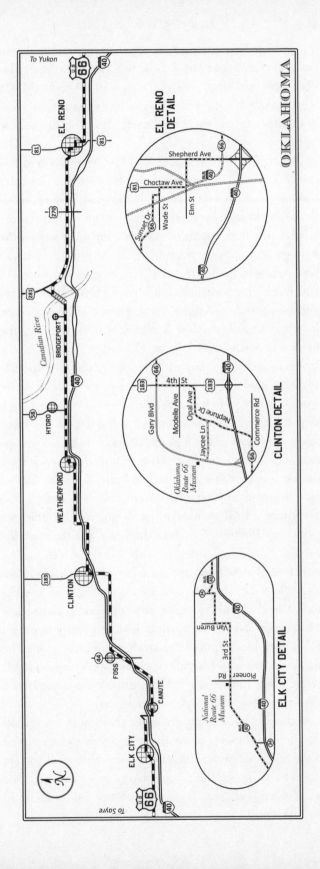

OKLAHOMA

To Yukon

EL RENO

EL RENO DETAIL

Shepherd Ave
Choctaw Ave
Sunset Dr
Wade St
Elm St

CLINTON DETAIL

4th St
Gary Blvd
Modelle Ave
Opal Ave
Neptune Dr
Jaycee Ln
Commerce Rd
Oklahoma Route 66 Museum

Canadian River
BRIDGEPORT
HYDRO
WEATHERFORD
CLINTON
FOSS
CANUTE
ELK CITY

To Sayre

ELK CITY DETAIL

Van Buren
3rd St
Pioneer Rd
National Route 66 Museum

At Wade Street, turn west again, then north and continue west on Sunset Drive. Bear right just after the sign for Fort Reno and short of the entrance to westbound I-40. Another quick right will take you up to Fort Reno itself. But unless a special event is planned, there is little cause to linger.

Heading west, you'll have a choice. You may continue due west on the 1932 alignment or turn north on an older route for Calumet and Geary. Unless you have plenty of time, the straight-west route may be better. Beyond the US 270 junction, continue west, bearing northwest at the Y intersection. Follow Spur 281 to the next Y and bear west-southwest onto US 281. Then, be ready for a treat as you approach a pony truss bridge of no fewer than thirty-eight—count 'em—thirty-eight spans. The bridge's span over the Canadian River is almost 4,000 feet, and the deck was opened to traffic in 1933. It is also one of the landmarks in John Ford's 1940 film *The Grapes of Wrath*.

There are lots of roadie explanations for the number of spans here: frequent washouts, the weight of tank convoys, a steel shortage, and so on. But the truth is that each of these spans is as large as the highway department's early equipment could lift into place. Of course you can stick with the tank convoy story if it works better for you. Part of traveling is taking home whatever stories you like.

Where US 281 turns south, continue west to **Bridge-port** and **Hydro**. Take care, however, for the road has several dipsy doodles through this section, which may be punctuated by unexpected stretches of gravel. There are a couple of old live-over gas stations along here as well, including Lucille's, perhaps now operating under new ownership. But it's the road itself that is really the main attraction here—pink tree-shaded concrete with the innocent-looking little half curbs that were once so innovative. The trouble was that the curbs accomplished more than was intended by highway engineers.

Instead of promoting drainage, they could turn a hill face into a solid sheet of water during a downpour—which is the only kind of rain Oklahoma seems to have. If you got between two such hills, you'd likely stay there until the weather cleared. Sometimes other folks would come slithering down to the bottom, too, making an even bigger mess.

A second purpose of the curbs was to redirect errant autos back onto the roadway. The curbs managed that, too. But many cars were flipped over in the process. Not surprising that you don't see a lot of this kind of curbing anymore.

Approaching **Weatherford** on the north service road of I-40, make a quick jog south onto westbound Main Street via Washington Avenue. To the north a few blocks is Southwestern Oklahoma State University. Overlooking the town, the site is all the more attractive for its early architecture, recalling the days when it served as a teachers college. The campus remains one of the prettiest anywhere along the route.

Departing Weatherford, continue straight west as the state highway curves southwest, and turn south on 4th Street / SR 54. Follow the sharp bend west and continue on old Route 66 on the north side of I-40. Slowing for some really evil speed bumps, cross under at the intersection and turn west at the stop, continuing on the south side beyond the next interchange.

Return to the north side as necessary and continue on the four-lane into **Clinton**. For the city route, turn south on 4th Street, then bend west on Opal Avenue, following Neptune Drive as far as an optional—and strongly recommended—route west on Jaycee Lane that will put you just south of the Oklahoma Route 66 Museum on Gary Boulevard. This was one of the first true museums dedicated to the old highway and remains one of the best.

Most Elvis sightings on old Route 66 have a distinct UFO quality, but you really can sleep in a room where Elvis stayed, at the Trade Winds Courtyard Inn. Or if Elvis isn't your style, they might have a Patsy Cline Room. You could ask. Either way, it's a good overnight.

Leaving Clinton, you face a definite history-or-food choice. To follow old Route 66, return to Neptune Drive and head west on Commerce Road / SR 66.

But if your lip is set for a world-class barbecue sandwich on a bun the size of Delaware, make tracks for the interstate and Jiggs Smokehouse. Jiggs used to advertise on a billboard along the highway, but most of the sign fell down some time ago. Didn't matter, though. The place is so well known now that customers from both coasts show up regularly for their barbecue fix. Even grab-it-and-go people, who don't usually notice their food or care that much for barbecue, end up way down the highway, licking the waxed paper and regretting the miles. Jiggs is on the north side of I-40 at the Parkersburg Road exit just west of Clinton. Come set a spell.

West Commerce Road leads to **Foss**, where you may continue on the north service road, crossing under I-40 the south side to **Canute**, a ghost town in the making. If you are a cemetarian, little Canute has a fine one with a sweet grotto, built in 1928 and well kept. Just west of town cross under the interstate again to the north side and continue west.

Enter **Elk City** on Business 40, jog north to the intersection with SR 34, then due south again. Head west to Van Buren and turn south again to 3rd Street.

If it's anywhere near lunchtime—or even if it isn't—you'll want to stop at the Country Dove, a gift shop and tearoom extraordinaire at 610 West 3rd Street. Oklahoma is not, as you may have discovered, a souper's paradise. But even if a light vegetarian lunch rings no bells for you, the French Silk Pie will. This dessert is so light, it's like sampling chocolate air, and it will leave you wondering whether you should use a fork or just smear it on yourself. Excellent food and fine hometown service.

Just beyond Pioneer Road, at 2717 West Third Street, is the National Route 66 Museum—another winner—with its neon Route 66 sign and two kachinas to welcome you. And this museum has something no other has: at present, the tallest oil derrick on Route 66, at 179 feet.

To continue on the old alignment, jog right onto the north frontage road just before the I-40 entrance, crossing under to the south side after four and a half miles and crossing over to the north side at Cemetery Road. Continue on into **Sayre**, turning right at the stop onto Business Loop 40. Through Sayre, bear south on Fourth Street / US 283. A jog west on Main Street will take you past the Beckham County courthouse, a classic in its design and also seen in *The Grapes of Wrath*. Return to Fourth Street and follow it directly across the Red River. The route to the older bridge, now impassable, is shown as optional.

It was at the old Route 66 bridge in Sayre that the Great Indian Uprising of 1959 is said to have occurred. The bridge itself had burned and was barricaded. But as each out-of-state car slowed for the detour, Sayre high school students excitedly told the tourists to roll up their windows and head west as fast as possible because Indians had burned the bridge and were on the warpath. For the better part of a day, the Oklahoma Highway Patrol had its hands full stopping all the speeding cars headed west to safety from all those rampaging Indians.

Heading west at a more leisurely pace, turn onto the north frontage road a mile beyond the present bridge, crossing under I-40 to the south side and continuing west into **Erick**. This pleasant, helpful town also had a speeding problem, but it was no joke. In fact, Erick had become known as one of the worst speed traps in the nation. Using a speedy black 1938 Ford with Oklahoma overdrive, Officer Elmer could catch just about anyone he had a mind to. When he once busted Bob Hope, the comedian quipped on his next radio show that the only way he'd go through Erick again would be on a donkey.

But Officer Elmer's prowess soon proved too much for the town. Tourist business fell badly, and Elmer had to go—at least officially. But on dark nights, speeding travelers along this stretch of road say that an old black Ford V-8 still has a way of mysteriously appearing in the rearview mirror. Just a warning, perhaps.

Farther down the road in **Texola**, it was a different tale. A few years before, there had been travelers and truck drivers all over the place, but the town was never considered boisterous. Folks were awakened one morning to find that some pranksters had climbed up to a huge TEXOLA sign facing onto the highway. There they'd simply changed the T to an S. Within hours, strangers were making purchases just to ask where the house (as in *cathouse*) was located.

Only a foundation remains where the welcoming sign with the saucy message once stood. But if you scrunch up

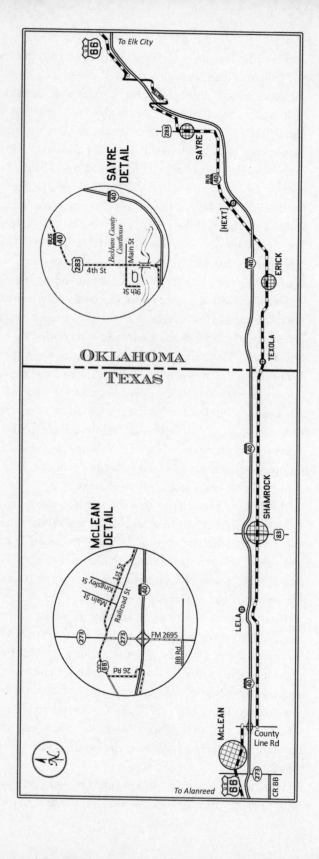

your eyes a little, it's not hard to imagine how inviting that sign must have looked to someone long on the road.

Texola is an interesting place to poke about, but even the old territorial jail is without customers.

TEXAS

Without a river or some continental rift, border crossings between states usually pass without notice. But not here. Almost immediately after entering Texas, the land changes. It's almost as if someone looked carefully at this place and decided, without regard for political interests, that the state line just naturally belonged right here.

As you leave the rolling, wooded hills of Oklahoma, the Panhandle of Texas opens like an immense natural stage. In the space of a few miles the land becomes flatter, more angular, a little more threatening. Not a good place to have a horse pull up lame if you were a line rider. Not a good place to have your old truck throw a rod if you were an Okie family trying with your little ones to reach California. Not a gentle place at all. But a place magnificent, like the sea, in its sheer, endless expanse. And in the way the land challenges you to open yourself to it, to take it all in—or to scuttle quickly across to an easier region.

Few places in America scrape at primitive human emotions the way Texas does. People who live on this land are afflicted either with a fierce loyalty known only to those who have learned to hold adversity lightly in their hands, or the equally burning desire to get the hell out.

Even the remnant of old Route 66 has a hunkered-down look as it climbs toward the breaks just west of Alanreed. Beyond these crumbling bluffs the high plains begin in earnest. A few miles more and the tumbled character of the land disappears almost completely, surrendering to a vast, treeless plain that flattens the entire horizon all the way into New Mexico. The distances seem endless:

> *The sun has riz,*
> *The sun has set,*
> *And here we is*
> *In Texas yet.*

So convinced were the earliest travelers that they were in imminent danger of becoming lost to death out here that they drove stakes into even the slightest rise to point the way. Coming upon these frail markers, riders from the south named this region Llano Estacado—the Staked Plain.

As you cross this land now with relative ease, imagine yourself out here alone, in an earlier time. Stakes or no, could you have walked this 200-mile stretch in search of something better than you had back home? Would you have done that? Interesting to notice what a tight grasp old Demon Comfort can have on us, isn't it?

But rather than just looking through the windshield at what lies everywhere around, take a few minutes out in the open along this stretch of road, or out near Adrian, beyond Amarillo. Walk for a bit, away from your car-cocoon and the certainty of a smooth, predictable highway. Even a few yards will do—toward whatever spot calls to you.

Get acquainted with the wind. No words, no other medium, can convey what earlier passers-through must have felt here on this land. But the wind still communicates it perfectly. So find that spot, walk out to it, and clear your mind for a few minutes. Notice what you're feeling as you stand facing into a wind older that the plain itself. Take just a moment to know something of this land before you move on. Sense what it means to be out here.

In Texas.

Shamrock to Adrian

Continue on the south service road from Texola, entering **Shamrock** on Business Loop 40. At the junction with US 83, be sure U Drop Inn, as the name has always suggested, and you'll find a friendly spot for a coffee break. You'll also discover that the Tower Service Station complex, dating from 1936, is perhaps the finest example of Art Deco architecture on all of old Route 66. Once crumbling, both the former Conoco station and adjoining café have been lovingly restored by dedicated local citizens—the tower is even outlined by neon against nighttime skies. Green derby hats off to Irish Shamrock. And if the building looks familiar, its look-alike appeared in the feature film *Cars*.

West of Shamrock is **Lela**, a tiny left-behind village. Yet it has the distinction of being a town on its way down that's now on the way up. Founded in 1902 as a rail station, the town soon had a post office, a newspaper, and several businesses. But by the thirties students were attending Shamrock schools, and the businesses began pulling out. In 1947, the population dropped to 50 or less. Thirty years later, the post office was closed. Yet the 1970 census put the population at 112, and by 2000 the town had grown to 135 residents. What do you suppose the next census will show?

Continuing west, take the south service road, cross I-40 at County Line road, and enter **McLean** on First Street / Main Street. McLean is one of the nicer towns in the Panhandle, however, so don't hurry. Life is slower paced here. On Sunday morning, people on the way to church all take care to wave hello to a stranger. Small towns like this were once the extended families of America. McLean still is.

Like many Panhandle towns, McLean has suffered from a roller-coaster oil business (pronounced *awl bidness* in Texan) as well as being bypassed by the interstate. But townspeople are preserving McLean's ties to the old road. At the east end of town, a Sears bra factory has become a barbed wire (pronounced *bob war*) museum with a walk-through Route 66 display. At the west end, there's a vintage Phillips 66 station and tanker truck. Farther along, you'll find the Cactus Inn, refurbished and ready for guests.

Departing McLean, you'll have an opportunity to experience another old, old dirt section of the route, with its companions: a section of derelict Route 66 and an abandoned bit of railway roadbed. Just turn south on SR 273 and west on County BB through a sharp jog and several bends to Main and Third Street in **Alanreed**. It's a special drive for the curious and purists. Inquire locally about road conditions, though, and don't even *consider* it during or after rain.

To continue on pavement, follow the north frontage road from McLean as it crosses to the south side of I-40. You'll be riding on a section of the old Route 66 four-lane, also toward Alanreed. There it's best to rejoin I-40. Take exit 124 to cross over on SR 70 and turn for a short run into **Groom**. Relics there still exist but are being carted away. At 407 East Front Street, the Golden Spread Grill has been serving travelers and locals for years. When the noon siren blows, everyone in town seems to show up.

Nearby, to the north, the Britten USA water tower is sure to get your attention, just as intended. How many tourists do you suppose bought a little of this or that when they stopped to ask about this Leaning Tower of Texas? It's marketing in the best roadside tradition and also made its way into *Cars*.

Heading west you'll pass through **Conway** and join Farm-to-Market Road (FM) 2161 to approach **Amarillo**. Cross under I-40 shortly after and continue west on FM 2575, skirting the south of Amarillo International Airport and turning north on Avenue B to take East Amarillo Boulevard / Business 40 into the city.

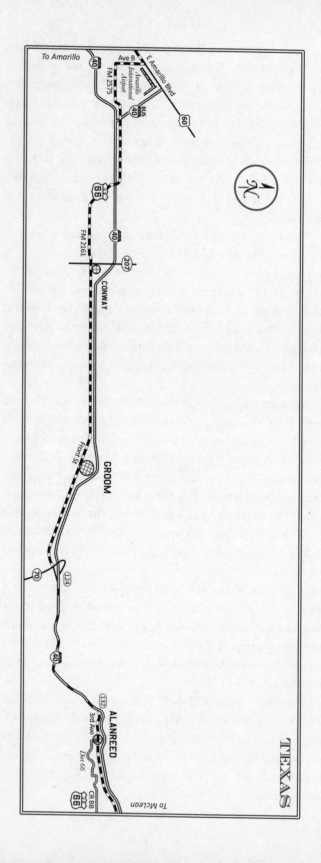

There's a strong feeling of the old flat road along here, though it can reflect tough times out on the edge of town. Don't sell Amarillo short, though. It's one of the most underrated cities along old Route 66 and well worth a tour through town and a special stop in the 6th Street area between Georgia and Western Streets.

Part of the original route is now one-way, so to follow it from Business 40, turn south on Taylor Street and then west again onto 6th Street. This neighborhood is a great comeback story in itself. Instead of urban blight, you'll now find a mile-long stretch of successful Route 66–era businesses. Plan your strategy over a traditional chili-and-cheeseburger at Golden Light Café, in an unpretentious brick building at 2906 Southwest 6th Street. The place dates from 1946 and is on the National Register of Historic Places. Then fan out to cover the delightful boutiques, antique shops, bookstores, and clubs you'll find along here. If you're there in the evening, Golden Light Cantina is right next door—open weekends with live entertainment.

Originally this area was part of the suburb of San Jacinto Heights, and it still bears some of the feeling of Texas towns where the Bible Belt runs head-on into the Wild West tradition. Rooming houses employing, according to one Amarillo city official, "ladies of whenever" were sometimes exorcised when the property changed hands in order to drive off whatever naughty spirits might remain. Yet while they operated, these houses

were accepted in a neighborhood of family-owned businesses.

Not far away, at 2705 6th Street, the Amarillo Natatorium awaits restoration. It once offered indoor swimming
as a temporary respite from summertime heat. Truly a
Panhandle phenomenon, the Nat looked like an architectural Appaloosa horse—with a graystone Moorish-Camelot
front half—joined to a porthole-dotted steamship. Although the pool concept didn't pan out, the Nat did become an outstanding attraction as a ballroom. Reopening
in 1926 (the same year in which Route 66 was chartered),
the Nat hosted the top bands of the thirties and forties—
Paul Whiteman, Count Basie, Louis Armstrong, Benny
Goodman, and Harry James. Not bad for an old swimming hole.

But West 6th Street's place in history was ensured by
its Texas-style shoot-from-the-hip marketing. During
hard times, one grocer took to announcing his daily spe-
cials to shoppers from the rooftop of his building. And the
way he got the crowd's attention was by tossing live chickens off the roof. Now, while it's a fact that chickens in
their natural state can do a little flying, these were
market-ready, clipped-wing models with all the flight
characteristics of a feathered rock. From the roof, about
the best anyone could expect was a barely controlled free
fall. So if you were headed for this grocery, you had to be
prepared. And you probably had to like chicken stew. The
Chicken Follies are gone now—just as well.

Jogging southwest on Bushland Boulevard and then
west on 9th Avenue, continue on out of town on Business
40. West of Amarillo, old Route 66 exists as the north service road for I-40, just a few yards away, so there is little
advantage in taking the old road with its frequent stop
signs and careless pickup trucks.

Yet west of Amarillo, on the south side at Exit 62, keep
watch for a row of ten Cadillacs—in various stages of
fin—augered methodically into the land just south of the
interstate. Although the installation looks like something
left by Druids, Cadillac Ranch was in fact placed here by
Pop Art financier Stanley Marsh 3. It may also be the clearest visual statement ever about wretched excess in oil-
propelled America. Try as we will to ignore the message of

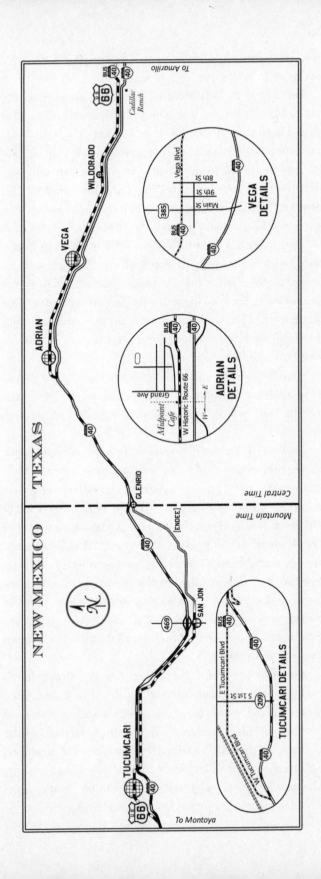

these iron dinosaurs, we cannot. Change your ways, they say in mute eloquence, or join us.

Farther west, **Wildorado**, despite an enticing name, is less than its former self. **Vega** is a different story and is dialed in to its Route 66 heritage. In town, the Best Western Sands is a pleasant family-run motel—with enduring status—out away from the city. or if staying in authentic places warms your heart, try the Vega Motel on Route 66 at US 385. It's an original, including those old in-between garages, plus furnishings from the 1940s.

For food, it's Boot Hill Saloon & Grill at 909 Vega Boulevard, with western-tinged entrées from fired calf to pan-seared tilapia, all from the enchanting mind of Chef Rory. Or consider Hickory Grill, a bit farther on, at 1004 Vega Boulevard, also well recommended. And you thought Chicago was hot . . . Here comes the West, kiddo. Even the menus tell you so.

Also be sure to check out the restored 1924 Hi-Way Magnolia Service Station that opened its doors on the Ozark Trail before Route 66 was slated to pass through here.

Now we get down to some really serious road stuff. Along this section of highway, keep an eye out for the Mid-Point water tower, next, in **Adrian**. Based on averages—summarized in the Route 66 Mileage Table at the back of this book—Adrian is at the the geo-mathematical center of old Route 66 as you've been driving it. And with the technology available today, new measurements have been averaged in, with the result that the centerline can be more accurately stated: it is not only in Adrian, but appears to run right through the Midpoint Cafe, an all-time great place for breakfast and lunch. Open seven days a week. Closed January and February.

Ever had ugly-crust pie to start the day? If not, here's your chance. The Midpoint Cafe is already a legend along Route 66 and has been featured on a number of travel and food shows, plus the movie *Cars*. So throw yourself a little celebration there. It's a friendly place featuring good food served with a smile. In addition to the adjoining gift shop, the cafe features a wide range of Route 66 goodies. And say Ha—that's Texan for Hi—to owner Fran when you mosey in. As locals will tell you: *When you're here, you're halfway there.*

Beyond Adrian the old road continues for a short distance before you rejoin the interstate headed for the Glenrio exit on the New Mexico border.

NEW MEXICO

New Mexico is descended from the sky. Other places along old Route 66 have been formed from rivers, mountains, and plains. Other states have been forged by iron-willed men meeting in urgency behind closed doors to make a truce, a compromise, a set of defensible boundaries. But New Mexico has no door on its history, no roof on its being. The first allegiance of most people here is to the land and to the generous sky above. Boundaries here seem best determined where these two—earth and sky—meet.

In the New Mexican view, cities are to be used as gathering points—for art as much as commerce—and not for population centers or power bases. Santa Fe is older than any city of Colonial America and has been a capital for more than three hundred years, yet its population barely tops 75,000. The oldest public building in the United States is right here in Santa Fe. Yet even with such a head start, the city withstood the push for a city proper airport until recently—and it's a good bit out of town. Newcomers rarely understand this until they have stayed here for a while. Then they realize why there was for so long no major airline operation in Santa Fe. . . . It would interfere with the sky.

In New Mexico, travelers along old Route 66 begin to notice something different in the sky above about the time they reach Tucumcari. The color—a deeper, more translucent lens of cobalt blue—can take even experienced color photographers by surprise. No wonder the painters, and after them the writers, began migrating here well before Route 66 first made its way across the state. Driving through New Mexico's high country in crackling bright sunshine, or rolling along one of the long valleys, with billowing rain clouds so close overhead they seem almost touchable, everything here seems to put you at stage center. You always seem to be right in the middle of the performance. And you are.

It's easy for a traveler to get religion—any kind—in a place like New Mexico, where earth and sky and wind and water greet one another in such unexpected ways. All the simple distinctions of mind, former notions about what is and what isn't, begin to blur. When you follow old Route 66 at a slower pace through the eastern hills, across the Continental Divide and into tabled mesa country, your perceptions change. It's easier here, as an observer, to become part of all that is observed, to feel a sense of connection with everything around. As a traveler, it is easier to slip loose from the sense of detachment and not-belonging that often seems to be a part of any great crossing.

This enchanted land asks little of you as a traveler, except one thing. It asks that you allow yourself to become enchanted, too.

Glenrio to Tucumcari

The town of **Glenrio** is another place that lost its starch when the interstate blazed through. Although the sign for a business loop through Glenrio may be somewhat misleading,

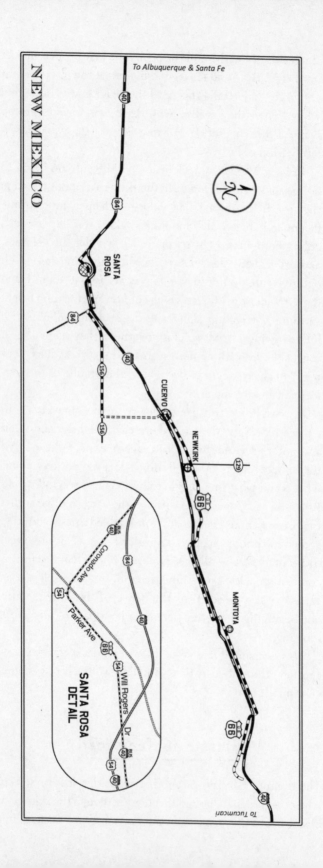

this nearly empty town remains a charming vestige along old Route 66. The well-known Last Motel in Texas / First Motel in Texas flourished just east of the state line. But its sign has faded and fallen, along with the hopes and dreams of another bypassed town. Just past the middle of town, though, you'll slip from Central to Mountain Time, gaining an hour in the blink of an eye.

West of Glenrio, the 1950s route continues on the north side of I-40 from Exit 369 to 356, but the interstate is okay for a few miles. For the more adventurous, during dry weather, the old road does continue on into **San Jon** as a dirt and gravel track of some eighteen miles. At San Jon, return to the old road on the south side and continue west toward **Tucumcari**, crossing under I-40 to the north side and entering town on Tucumcari Boulevard / Business 40.

For most old-time Route 66 travelers, the mythical West began with some simple but meaningful event. For many it was the first glimpse of a long, low fencelike sign for Whiting Brothers—an independent chain that at one time numbered 150 or more gas stations. For others, it was the signs of Tucumcari. CITY OF 2,000 ROOMS. THE ONLY PLACE TO SPEND TONIGHT. With such powerful roadside advertising, Tucumcari was tough to pass by, and few did. Here you'll see many survivors: The Tee Pee, Blue Swallow, Palomino. Sweet reminders, still among us and valued by all who travel old Route 66.

Tucumcari to Santa Rosa

As you head west, road conditions require that you return to I-40 through the stretch from west of Tucumcari to Exit 321. Exiting south, an old section turns east to a dead end. To continue west, follow the south service road past **Montoya** through **Newkirk** to **Cuervo**—three dear but near-death towns, strung out along the old road like amulets on an antique Spanish chain.

Sections of the old highway through this region are often part of very old routes, predating the first New Mexico road begun with federal aid, back in 1918. The tiny grocery stores that came later were not only tourist stops but the center of life here, connecting travelers, townspeople, and those who roamed these *barrancas*, even before the Spanish arrived. Richardson's Store & Good Gulf, Knowles Grocery, and Wilkerson's—all became way stations for later long-haul rigs, touring cars, ponies, and school buses. But like the hand-painted signs on the old clapboard siding, they are fading fast. It's also an easy section to follow, from one side of the interstate to another, like a slow dance step across time and memory.

From **Cuervo**, the interstate west is easier. But the original alignment can be followed south from town over County Road 2C, a 5-mile gravel stretch to SR 156, then east over pavement to US 84. This is a wonderful section of the old two-lane with much of the feel of Route 66 across New Mexico during the 1930s and 1940s—open, free of commercial development, and wild. Especially wild.

After turning west onto SR 156, you'll notice the small animals and birds by the thousands inhabiting the ground cover closing in on both edges of the highway. So please, if you drive this section, don't exceed 35 to 40 miles per hour. Many creature-generations have passed since these roadside inhabitants were traffic-wise. And they are part of what makes this segment of Route 66 special. Give them the benefit of your choice to drive this section with extra care.

From SR 156, jog north on US 84, passing under I-40 to enter **Santa Rosa** on Will Rogers Drive. Santa Rosa is also a Route 66 landmark. But unlike Tucumcari, it needed far less advertising. Santa Rosa has the weather on its side. More people have been snowbound in Santa Rosa than almost anywhere west of St. Louis. And it's a pretty good place to be stranded. For years, it was the home of the Club Cafe, known for its biscuits and gravy as well as the satisfied-looking Fat Man on billboards along Route 66.

With sparse automobile traffic and few bus stops to speak of, the Club Cafe finally closed. But its spirit has been preserved by the owners of Joe's Bar & Grill Cantina, formerly Joseph's Bar & Grill, right on the route at 865 Will Rogers Drive. Good food served with care for travelers. Snowing or not, be sure to stop in.

Santa Rosa North and West

You'll have a major choice along I-40 just beyond Santa Rosa. One route takes you through Santa Fe; the other heads west into Albuquerque. Both have sections of old Route 66, though for scenery and culture Santa Fe wins in a walk. The maps on pages 80 to 82, show how both routes fit together with Route 66 through Albuquerque and beyond.

Santa Rosa to Santa Fe

If Santa Fe is your preference, turn north on US 84 west of Santa Rosa, which joins the old Route 66 alignment to the north. Note: Should you miss the turn (or change your mind), exit I-40 at SR 3 northbound. It's beautiful country and a fine wiggly road past Villanueva State Park, connecting with Route 66 just east of San Jose. You won't miss much and will feel like an adventurer on this trek north that few but the locals know.

Along US 84, which becomes old Route 66 after a few miles, you'll continue on to **Romeroville**. From there, turn southwest to follow Route 66, also known as Las Vegas Highway, along a 46-mile loop swinging northwest past **Tecolote**, **Serafina**, and **Bernal**. Continue on, over and under the interstate beyond **Rowe** into **Pecos** on SR 63. Continuing southwest on SR 50, you must re-join I-25 briefly. Take Exit 294 at **Cañoncito** to rejoin the route north on Pecos Trail to **Santa Fe**. This city is unique, so plan to spend some time here. There are so many fine restaurants and galleries, you could easily eat and art yourself into oblivion.

Santa Fe is a close-together city, with narrow non-RV streets—it's been here since 1609 or so—and the inevitable one-ways believed by some to ease congestion. So it's useful to choose whether Route 66 through the city or Santa Fe itself tops your agenda. Compromise can be tough to achieve—imagine American-style traffic poured into a Spanish village.

Our tour here is a simple one, to be adjusted as needed. It is a passage through town on remnants of Route 66,

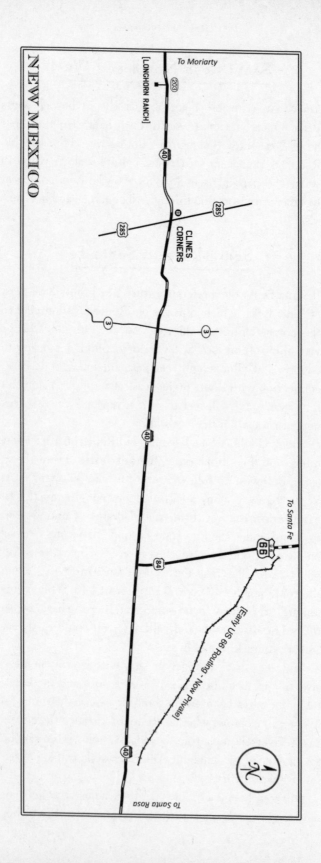

NEW MEXICO

To Moriarty

[LONGHORN RANCH]

203

40

285

285

CLINES CORNERS

3

3

40

To Santa Fe

66

84

[Early US 66 Routing - Now Private]

40

To Santa Rosa

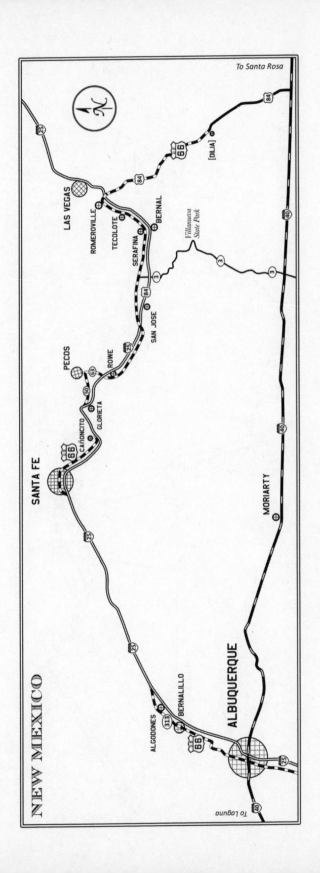

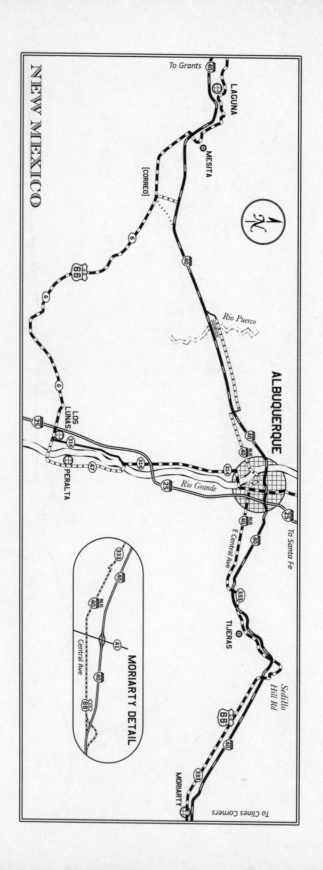

SANTA FE DETAIL

plus a few highlights. Historic Route 66 signs are posted, yet these can be misleading. Check the suggested route against the map a time or two before entering the city and plan to check in with the visitor center at 491 Old Santa Fe Trail, just north of Paseo de Peralta, near the New Mexico state capitol. Information gained there can make your entire visit more enjoyable—and relaxed.

From the south, follow Old Las Vegas Highway / SR 300. Continue straight on Old Pecos Trail / SR 466 as SR 300 bears left. Bear right on Old Pecos Trail as SR 466 goes left and Route 66 becomes Old Santa Fe Trail. Your heads-up will be De Vargas Street for a left turn on East Alameda Street. Watch at Don Gaspar for a right turn onto northbound Galisteo Street. Turn right on West Water Street, recross Don Gaspar (are you having fun yet?), and continue on to a right turn on Old Santa Fe Trail, with another right onto East Alameda Street. At Galisteo, turn left for a short section of two-way traffic leading to a right bend onto Cerrillos Road, the old route out of town. There, you've done it, and have a better idea of how the city works.

For an overnight, you may as well continue on for a few minutes to El Rey Inn at 1862 Cerrillos Road. The place has become a Route 66 icon—prior reservations advised—expanding from a small motel early on, to the enjoyable complex it is today. Well recommended, with fireplace rooms, an early-getaway breakfast, and a family-owned feel to the place. Good place for touring advice as well.

In town, as you'd imagine, prices are well up there. At the top end, little can compare to the Inn of the Five Graces at 150 East De Vargas Street. Less stratospheric, yet still a model of design and comfort, is Inn on the Alameda at 303 East Alameda Street. If life (and shopping) on the Plaza attracts, La Fonda on the Plaza, at 100 East San Francisco Street, could do it for you.

Whether you stay in town or not, leave ample time for a visit to the plaza—no charge for browsing. And if churches and mystery interest you, Loretto Chapel is a charming stop. The rest you'll find on your own with the handful of brochures you already have.

Take time, if you can, for a good look at the state capitol. It has been designed to incorporate the Zia, New Mexico's ancient sun symbol (see below), with the four seasons of the year, four periods of the day, four stages of life, and the four points of the compass. All of life is at work here, in this ancient symbol, as it has been for well over six hundred years. Something to consider as you drive south into Zia Pueblo country.

Santa Fe to Albuquerque

Heading out of town on Cerillos Road, join I-25 south. Farther on, take the **Algodones** exit for Route 66 / SR 313 through **Bernalillo** and **Alameda**. Nearing Albuquerque, the road curves into 4th Street NW. If you haven't done so, it's wise to stop along here to check your map and be sure where you'll be headed, once into the center of Albuquerque. That done, continue south, jog east on Roma Avenue, and turn south again for a short distance to Central Avenue. Here you may turn east to visit Albuquerque highlights—and neon—or west toward Old Town.

Santa Rosa to Albuquerque

If you've chosen the direct route to Albuquerque via **Clines Comers**, **Moriarty**, and **Tijeras**, continue west from Santa Rosa on I-40. Consider taking a moment for Longhorn Ranch at Exit 203. Although not typical of early mom-and-pop attractions, the Longhorn does sport some of the carnival feeling of the old route.

Returning to the interstate, continue to the Moriarty exit and follow the old route on Business 40 through town. A lone survivor of the Whiting Brothers chain of gasoline stations is still operating there and will hopefully be hanging on when you roll into town. Beyond Moriarty, continue west on SR 333. Take Exit 181 for the Sedillo Hill Road section of the old road, pass under I-40, and continue on through Tijeras. From there, you'll pass over I-40 and connect with East Central Avenue / Business 40 leading into Albuquerque.

Both the old highway and the newer interstate look easily laid out through this area, but that is part of the road builder's art. Because Tijeras Canyon was such tough going, new construction has often been delayed on this section. Consider a report from the New Mexico Highway Department from as late as 1951. It described the result of setting off dynamite charges in a thousand holes that had been laboriously drilled in one small area. That's a thousand charges set off simultaneously. One helluva bang, all right. But here's the clincher. After all that, there was so little debris that it took only twenty minutes to clear it all up. Very hard stuff around here.

If you've stayed on the interstate, you may exit for Business 40 at Central Avenue. However, there is very little feeling of old Route 66 along the eastern reaches of Central Avenue. A route that leaves more time for touring the downtown section is to exit at San Mateo Boulevard southbound and turn west again on Central Avenue. Local revitalization projects have done wonders to preserve and maintain charming shops and businesses in the downtown area. The 66 Diner at 1405 Central Avenue is a fine nouveau-fifties eatery. And Lindy's Coffee Shop has been serving terrific chili and other excellent fare since 1929. Always ready to serve hungry roadies, it's a tradition on Central at Fifth Street.

Motel properties have fared less well, though a few survivors like the De Anza and El Vado may still show wonderful neon. But for a truly special stay, the Andaluz Hotel—formerly La Posada—a block north of Central at 125 Second Street, has been lovingly restored and is the choice for romantic charm from bygone days. Each bar and restaurant reflects the 1930s New Mexican tone of the hotel. In all, the restoration revives Conrad Hilton's vision—a stay-forever, top-drawer place. It's difficult not to write whole paragraphs about it. See for yourself . . .

Another of Albuquerque's restorations is the lovely KiMo Theater, past the center of town. Originally built by the Boller Brothers, recognized in the Southwest for their Hi-Ho Rococo style, it now stands as a model of what can and should be accomplished all along old Route 66.

A visit to Albuquerque's Old Town is special. Here, in a walkable space, the past and present of arts and crafts marketing is mixed well with a sense of history.

Albuquerque to Laguna

If you are taking the southwestern section of old Route 66 / SR 6 via **Los Lunas**, jog west on Central Avenue and turn south again on 4th Street Southwest. Jog west on Bridge Boulevard to cross the Rio Grande, and south again on Isleta Boulevard / SR 314. Turn west on SR 6 to Los Lunas and continue on SR 6 toward Laguna. Or, if you are short on time, just take I-25 south to the SR 6 exit for the old Route 66 run northwest.

This route, with everything from near-zero traffic density to a row of baby volcanoes, is an exceptional drive in itself and also offers an occasional glimpse of old, old Route 66 on the south side. Whether you've been following the interstate or the old road, SR 6 from Albuquerque and Los Lunas to Correo is a fine section that can take you back in time to experience how it looked and felt to be westbound on Route 66 and almost entirely alone on the old two-lane . . . Except for the Santa Fe Railway—now the BNSF—with streamliners like the *Super Chief*, the Train of the Stars that ripped through here daily in both directions. And *ripped* is the right word, because there's a straight-shot section of track along here where the trains topped a hundred miles an hour—pretty good for the 1940s—in a blur of red, yellow, and silver.

Now only Amtrak's *Southwest Chief* and a host of freights lumber through here. Still, if you're close to the track, as this road so often is, and a freight comes along, give the engineer an arm-pump signal. There's a good chance the locomotive's horn will sound in reply. This is the stuff of good story-telling. Don't miss it.

For I-40 travelers taking the optional route from Albuquerque west, there's a special treat at the Rio Puerco crossing where a 1933 through-truss bridge is being preserved by the New Mexico State Highway Department. A grand place to poke around and take photographs.

Whether you've followed the SR 6 routing or I-40, a delightful bit of the old road—snaking around rocky

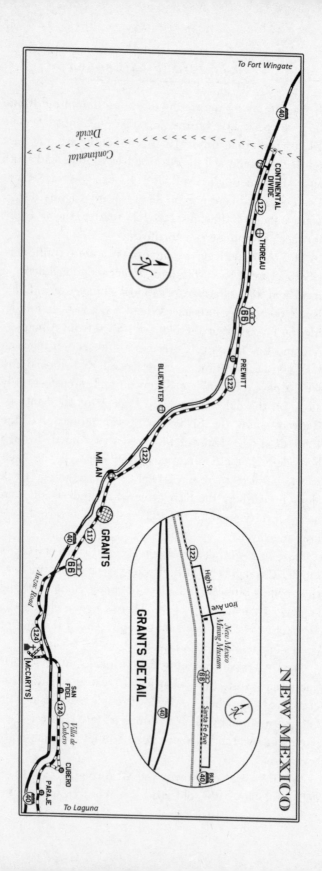

overhangs—awaits you near Exit 117 from **Mesita** to **Laguna**. Mesas, views, cottonwoods, lonely Santa Fe tracks to the north—these few miles are some of the most beautiful anywhere, and are best driven at a slow pace.

Keep a close watch for children playing and people walking along the road. This is part of the vast Laguna Reservation—stay on recommended roadways and refrain from taking photographs without permission. Treat this native land with the same respect due foreign soil. It is, and we are guests here.

Laguna to Continental Divide

Continue west past **Laguna** for another superb section of old Route 66. This stretch of road is a little slower than SR 6 from Los Lunas, but there's also much to be rediscovered here, so take your time though **Paraje** on SR 124 and up toward **Cubero**, on an optional section, to Villa de Cubero.

It was here that Ernest Hemingway settled in with his notebooks to write a major part of *The Old Man and the Sea*. At least that's what we all believed. But in a remarkable piece of literary research published in the spring 2008 issue of *American Road*, writer and preservationist Johnnie V holds that moth to a flame. Checking with several recognized Hemingway authorities, including Mike Reynolds, whose five-volume chronology of Hemingway's life is a mainstay in the field, it was quickly discovered that Hemingway's commute from Cuba to Idaho scarcely left any time at Villa de Cubero. Moreover, a signature claimed to be his does not appear to match those of letters and documents signed by Hemingway.

Is it possible that the Pulitzer and Nobel Prize–winning author did at least stay at Villa Cubero? It appears so. But to venture more than that would be to go against very long odds. Yet none of that changes the appeal of Villa de Cubero. How many places have you loved to visit where Hemingway did not write a book? Thousands? Well then, make this another. And add it to your personal list of Route 66 mysteries.

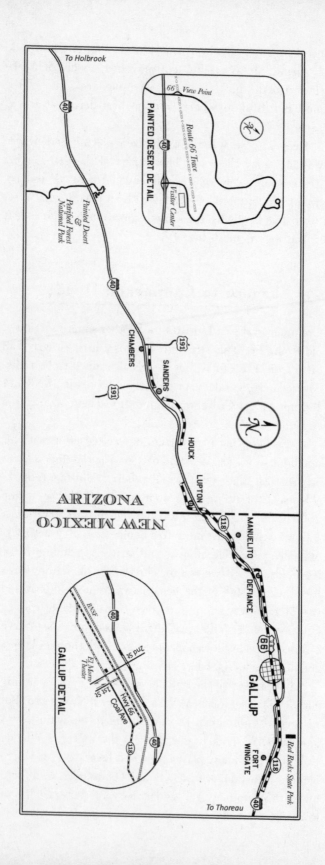

To Holbrook

PAINTED DESERT DETAIL

66 View Point

Route 66 Trace

Visitor Center

Painted Desert & Petrified Forest National Park

CHAMBERS

SANDERS

HOUCK

LUPTON

ARIZONA
NEW MEXICO

MANUELITO

DEFIANCE

GALLUP DETAIL

BNSF

2nd St

El Morro Theater

1st St

Hwy 66

Coal Ave

GALLUP

FORT WINGATE

Red Rocks State Park

To Thoreau

Crossing under I-40 to the south side, Route 66 / SR 124 continues, with an optional jog down past **McCartys**. Take Indian Service Road (ISR) 27 across ISR 30, where a lovely church surveys a near ghost town at its feet. Although this side trip appears to be sanctioned by the State of New Mexico, you will be on the Acoma Reservation. Take care not to trespass or take photographs while here. Reconnect with SR 124 by turning back toward the interstate on ISR 30.

A little farther west, choose Anzac Road, an old Route 66 alignment that will rejoin SR 124 to cross under I-40 and continue on the north side as SR 117 into **Grants**, one of the first towns along the highway in New Mexico to embrace the idea of a Route 66 revival. Stop by the visitor center at 515 High Street, a couple of blocks past 2nd Street, for information on history and local attractions, including the New Mexico Mining Museum. Uranium ore was big here back in the 1950s, during the cold war. But hard-rock mining is the same anywhere—isolated and dangerous. The museum conveys that.

And if you're among the many who are traveling in summer, you may want to head south from Grants to the perpetual Ice Caves, where the temperature never rises above 31°F. Even if you've already done some caving, you'll find this attraction to be different.

From Grants, the old road continues as SR 122 through **Milan**, past **Bluewater**—the spiritual home of American hubcaps and worth a stop—**Prewitt**, and **Thoreau** (pronounced locally as *Threw*) and on to the town of **Continental Divide**.

There, along the north side, on Route 66, continue straight ahead for a bit and you'll be on the geographic cusp of the Continental Divide. Stretch for a bit, think of rivers flowing in opposite directions from the wavy line down the mountain chain from where you stand, and get an Intrepid Explorer photo of yourself next to the sign. It's good fun!

Continental Divide to State Line

Return to I-40 for just over ten miles, then take the exit for **Iyanbito**. Continue along SR 118 on the north side, past **Fort Wingate** and Red Rock State Park, where a portion of the first *Superman* was filmed. Enter **Gallup** on the main thoroughfare, marked Highway 66. More than most cities on the highway, Gallup maintains a sense of the Route 66 era. Little has been lost and, as the old alignment jogs south on First Street, then west on Coal Avenue before returning to Route 66, look for some of the fine old buildings like the Drake and Grand hotels and El Morro Theater, also designed by the Boller Brothers. Stop by the visitor center at 255 East Historic Highway 66 and ask for a guide to historic buildings when you arrive.

Gallup also has something few other places on Route 66 can claim—a longtime connection to Hollywood. The Gallup area has provided unequaled movie scenery for movies from *Redskin*, filmed in 1929, to the more recent adventures of *Superman*. And El Rancho Hotel, now beautifully and responsibly restored, was the on-location home to stars like Tracy and Hepburn, Bogart, Hayworth, Flynn, and Peck.

A production designer's dream, the hotel at first looks like an architectural collision between Mount Vernon and a backlot set for *Viva Villa*. There's even an Uncle Remus Wishing Well out front. Still, the overall effect is both inviting and absolutely right. How could it be otherwise? El Rancho, it has always been said, was designed for none other than R. E. Griffith, brother of the great film pioneer D. W. Griffith.

But hold the phone! There's a mystery brewing here. Exactly the kind of tale that the stars who stayed here and movie fans everywhere love. The truth is, D. W. Griffith never had a brother named R. E. Griffith. Those initials appear to belong instead to Raymond E. Griffith, a silent-film star turned comedy writer and producer.

R.E. had talent, no doubt about that, and was a production whiz, but he was also known in the industry as a pathological teller of tales, often making up outlandish stories just to see if he could get away with it. Or the obscure Mr. Griffith may have been another person altogether. But whatever his true identity, you've got to give the fellow credit. He put his D. W. Griffith story over on everyone for fifty years. So when you stay at El Rancho—and it's a must—drop by the taproom and hoist a glass to the memory of R. E. Griffith, who in death as in life damn near did fool all of the people all of the time.

Gallup remains a center for arts and crafts in New Mexico, so keep watch for some remarkable outdoor sculptures on the right, such as *Bebop,* which commemorates Route 66 and its neon, and the giant pottery bowl, with authentic Acoma paintings.

Also on the right, midway through town, is the Southwest Cultural Center, located on the second floor of the Santa Fe Railway depot, built in 1926. In addition to the walk-through displays in the center, you'll also find a charming deli restaurant reminiscent of the El Navajo, a well-known Fred Harvey hotel once sited here. The food is good and a player piano is on hand to entertain you. During the summer, Indian dance performances are given in a small amphitheater right next door. The shows are both exciting and free.

From Gallup, continue on Route 66, following SR 118 west past Fort Yellowhorse, which looks a lot like a movie set because that's what it was, having been built for the 1950 Kirk Douglas film *The Big Carnival.* Since then, the place has become a highway icon.

Continue on SR 118, crossing under I-40 to the south side west of Defiance, and under again to the north side past **Manuelito** toward the Arizona line. For years a great arch, supported by Eiffel Towerish strap-iron columns and topped by a large US 66 shield, stood astride the state border, wishing travelers well and asking them to come again. As with so many other simple things etched sharply in the common memory, the arch is gone now. Hardly even a photograph remains. But would it not be grand to create and preserve—for all those who will yet travel this road—a new archway in the same style?

There is a sign at the border, of course. But you pass through an arch and only go past a sign. It's a different feeling, passing under an arch—a feeling far more in tune with this old road and the way it conveys us, more gently somehow, from one state to the next.

CARTY'S CAMP

MODERN COTTAGES
East City Limits
NEEDLES, CALIFORNIA
W. R. CARTY, Proprietor

ARIZONA

Arizona is one of the youngest states in the Union, the last of the continental territories to be admitted, and one of the most thinly populated. Yet, Arizona can take care of itself, thank you very much.

That's the view of many folks along the route through the upper part of the state. It's been a useful attitude to have around here, too. Poor relation to the sprawling developments of southern Arizona (itself too often a poor cousin to Southern California), the northern part of the state has learned to light its own lamp, carry its own bucket.

A lot of folks living close by old Route 66 are transplants from other orphan regions—the Ozarks of Missouri or the panhandles of Oklahoma and Texas—and they know how the government-and-commerce game works: if you want to play ball, take the sprawl and all. Nothing doing, the people of northern Arizona have replied. Good for them.

This is harsh but beautiful country, the air clear and sharp, unspoiled for the most part. Mountains like the San Francisco Peaks rise spectacularly from a flattened landscape, allowing you to watch them come closer for hours before the highway finally curves around their base near the junction with US 89, the main north-south road.

Cattle are raised in northern Arizona, but it is not feed-and-ship cattle country so much as it is the true cowboy-and-Indian country of western legend. Zane Grey loved this land. He rode it and walked it and wrote about it. His was a special brand of romantic western—the kind where the hero still triumphs and rides through purple sage into a crimson sunset with his equally tough but tender sweet-heart. Over the years, nearly 150 million copies of Grey's books have been sold, with many made and remade into movies as well. So it is difficult to exaggerate the influence his notions of manhood, womanhood, and social justice have had on the American culture, and on anyone traveling old Route 66 across this land.

What's more, with the passage of two generations or so, the frontier is still very much a part of everything you'll find here. Stories of shoot-outs, lost gold mines, and desert massacres are still told by the people who lived through those days. It's a time warp worth stepping into.

There is also a compelling intimacy about the way old Route 66 and the land go on together. At night, especially, a personal feeling of timelessness is present here. Once you are away from the lights—east of Holbrook, up toward the Grand Canyon, or along the great northering swing west of Seligman—take time to stand for a while in the night. Pull the darkness around you like a cloak and feel what it is to be on the frontier of your own being, the land spilling away beyond your sight and hearing. Haul the stars down—so many here you may not even recognize old friends among them. Bring them close. Feel your own breathing and the life, unseen but sensed, everywhere around.

Not many places are left in which to take a moment like this. Northern Arizona, along old Route 66, is one of the last.

State Line to Holbrook

At the Arizona state line SR 188 ends and Route 66 continues as the frontage road on the south side of I-40, Route 66 / SR 118 passes through **Lupton**, on the border. The old roadbed ends west of Lupton and you must follow I-40 for a short time to the **Houck** exit. From there, you'll have short section of old Route 66. Then it's back up on the interstate to another brief section on the north side from **Sanders** to **Chambers** where the old road is only partially paved, with some gravel stretches. Mostly this is a section of lost towns: Cuerino, Navapache, and Goodwater. So unless you want to drive as much of Route 66 as possible, it's better to remain on the interstate beyond Lupton until you reach the exit for Painted Desert and Petrified Forest National Park. Of these, the Petrified Forest is more interesting to explore, with a good deal of old Route 66 flavor remaining. But the northern loop through Painted Desert has a nice pull-over area to view an old, old section of Route 66 right-of-way that once passed through here.

From Painted Desert, continue west on I-40. Creviced arroyos, long sloping rifts, grassy hardpan all around. This border region has a high-desert sweetness that can make you lightheaded with solitude. Sometimes, during a long driving day, a run through this country brings up an ancient German word *Fernweh*. It has no equivalent in English, but represents a longing for, a need to return to, a place you've never been.

Here, even on the interstate, you'll be reminded that it's in the nature of a desert to be harsh. But a sense of poignance is also present, especially along about sunset. So, if you've got a traveling-music collection, pull out a few tunes that bring you other voices, other times—that may even remind you of loves now gone separate ways—because this border region is special. It's a stretch where you can see yourself more clearly, hear the past more sweetly . . .

For **Holbrook**, take Exit 289 and enter on Navajo Boulevard / Business Loop 40. Turn west on Hopi Boulevard / Business Loop 40. Watch for the Pow Wow Trading

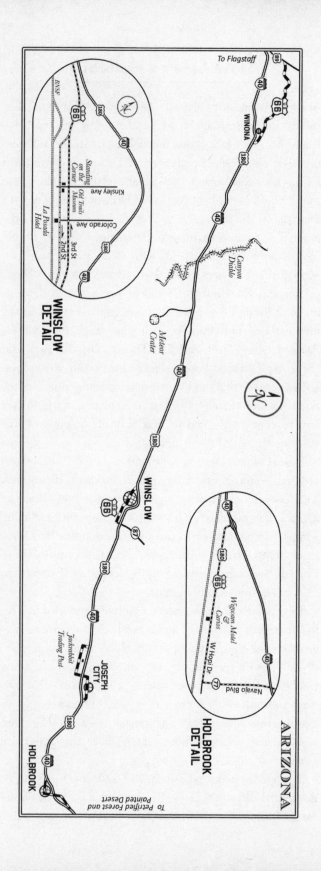

Post—really a wow if the neon is lit up at night—plus Joe and Aggie's Café, another Route 66 stalwart. And if you've always wanted to sleep in a teepee ("Oh, puh-leeze, can't we?"), Holbrook is the best place in the Southwest to do it. The design for Wigwam Village was patented in 1936, with the first units constructed in Kentucky and the Southeast. A similar tepee motel was also built on Route 66 in Rialto, California—so you'll have a second chance if the popular Holbrook Wigwams are booked. This is a place where it's a good idea to call ahead (928-524-3048).

Holbrook to Flagstaff

Rejoin I-40 / U.S. 180 west of Holbrook. This was once a touristy stretch of old Route 66, and some remnants like Geronimo's Trading Post have been surviving along the short section through **Joseph City**.

Now, maybe you can skip the sand paintings. But can you really go home without a rubber tomahawk? The Jackrabbit Trading Post—a major Route 66 icon—hangs in there, though, and probably has 'em. Recall all those yellow-and-black signs with the crouching rabbit that you've been seeing along the highway because . . . *here it is!* And definitely worth a stop, with a good feeling and an inventory right out of the 1940s. Cross I-40 west of Joseph City on Joe City Road and head west on Jackrabbit Road. The place will be pretty hard to miss.

Rejoin I-40 and continue on into **Winslow**, following Business Loop 40. Of the two major alignments through town, Second Avenue is best remembered, but at the one-way division you'll be shunted up onto Third Street. No matter. Just turn south on any street past North Kinsley Avenue, head back east on Second Street, and you'll catch the highlights.

Winslow was often remembered for two things: national roadside marketing and interesting ladies. Like Meramec Caverns and Jackrabbit, Winslow's Store for Men was one of the pioneers in roadside advertising. Its signature ads even wound up as far away as Paris and Guam. Store for Men was one of the rule-breakers, too. It was generally believed that billboards and bumper stickers might bring in travelers the first time but would not generate many return visits. Road-side ads were considered one-shots. But the Jackrabbit and Store for Men signs—which typically appeared together—pulled in the repeat business.

Winslow is remembered for a song as well. Roadies and locals often improved their prospects by getting duded up at the Store for Men before standing on a corner to wait for a girl (my lord) in a flatbed Ford. Eagles are nothing, you see, if not observant. A monument to the whole idea—Standin' on a Corner—is now immortalized in a statue and park on the northwest corner of Second Street and Kinsley Avenue.

Much of today's support for old Route 66 through Winslow first radiated from the Old Trails Museum, at 212 Kinsley Avenue. From years back, the museum led a movement to restore La Posada, a former Fred Harvey hotel now reopened and at the top of listings from travel publications and independent reviewers throughout the country.

Plan an overnight at La Posada, if you can, or take a meal in their wonderful restaurant, where they cook and bake from scratch for three meals daily. Their menu is extensive, not so pricey as you might imagine, since you'll be seated in the Turquoise Room—designed to re-create the private dining car of Santa Fe's *Super Chief*. As lodging and dining go along Route 66, La Posada tops both lists. At least wander there a bit to take in this extraordinary 1930 architectural design by Mary Colter, its history, and the care with which its owners have managed this magnificent restoration.

But all the historical action isn't just downtown. Across the tracks is the Winslow-Lindbergh Regional Airport. It was designed by Charles Lindbergh from his own experience in flying the mail, and named for him at a time when a string of beacons and airfields were in place all along Route 66 as airmail stops from Los Angeles to Chicago. Winslow was one of them. Lindbergh himself made the 1929 inaugural flight for Transcontinental Air Transport, later TWA. A photogenic hangar from the period still stands. The original 1932 terminal, with its dedication plaque, remains. And the E&O Kitchen housed in the building is a pleasant restaurant, locally owned, and serving good food.

Rejoin I-40 / US 180 for the run to meteor country—provide your own movie lead-in here . . . Around 50,000 years ago, a giant meteorite slammed into the Arizona desert with a force equal to some 20 million tons of high explosive. Happily, there was almost no one around here back then. Still, it must have been a helluva thump. Over the last century or so, its crater became a prime Route 66 curiosity, faded, and has now hit the comeback trail with a visitor center and amenities. The crater is about 6 miles south of the interstate—as if you're likely miss Exit 233!

Now make a beeline west to **Flagstaff**. There's plenty to see and do in this old lumbering center and university town. Great neon along motel row at night, too. Be sure to take the advice in Bobby Troup's song, though, and "don't forget Winona." It's a one-blink town, but when the trading post is open, the folks there have always been friendly and helpful. Winona is also the gateway to a beautiful drive through piñon country along the old alignment into Flagstaff. Take the Camp Townsend / Winona Road exit, continue to the junction with US 89, and turn south toward town.

Canyon Notes

Several splendid natural attractions are in this region: Grand Canyon to the west and Oak Creek Canyon to the south, paired with Sedona, red rock country, and Montezuma's Castle.

A less crowded approach to Grand Canyon's South Rim from Flagstaff is north via US 89. Or, if you love trains, the Grand Canyon Railway operates out of Williams.

On the South Rim, it's well worthwhile to stay or at least take a meal at El Tovar Hotel. This grand 1905 lodge—and a long-standing icon—at the canyon's edge speaks eloquently of days gone by. With Hopi House next door, the whole place smacks of oatmeal for breakfast and daily constitutionals. Teddy Roosevelt would have called it *bully,* and he'd be right. Plan well in advance, however; bookings can be tight year-round.

El Tovar was renovated in 2005 with such care that the sawyer who had cut the original barked siding came out of retirement to reface the lodge. The undertaking was so complex that to avoid any environmental disruption, the surrounding area was squared off with lines of string to enable Northern Arizona students to remove and replace—exactly—every plant that might be harmed. When the work was complete, a crowd stood by in tears as the last tiny plant was put back in its rightful place. That alone speaks volumes of the regard in which this property is held.

Whether you'll be visiting Grand Canyon this time or not, a marvelous day trip is the lovely drive south through Oak Creek Canyon and into old Sedona on SR 89A. While in the area take a couple of hours at the unusual cliff dwelling of Montezuma's Castle, an early Route 66 attraction still little changed from the time it was built a thousand years ago. And work in Boynton Canyon if you can. A return to Flagstaff on I-17 is easy and a time-saver.

Flagstaff is a mixed bag of old Route 66 survivors and new construction, yet its motel row and businesses retain much of the old-road feeling—like the Santa Fe freights that grumble and growl along just across the highway.

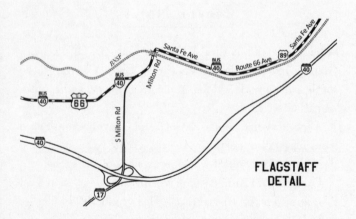

FLAGSTAFF
DETAIL

On the way into town take note of the Museum Club at 3404 East Route 66, a great place to scoot your boots and soak up some honky-tonk history. *Country America* named it the top dance club, and you can still hear echoes of stars like Willie Nelson and Waylon Jennings who played here. The National Register of Historic Places has listed the

Museum Club and the roadhouse has been on Route 66 since 1931.

In town, turn south from Route 66 onto original 66, now one-way Beaver Street, and east to the Flagstaff Visitor Center in the former Santa Fe Railway Depot at 1 East Route 66. A great place to begin your visit. If you catch them at off-hours, it's still a great place to connect with the spirit of Flagstaff.

For a moderately priced overnight hotel complex, Little America at 2525 East Butler Avenue east of town is reputable, or try the very nice Radisson Woodlands Plaza on the other end of town, at 1175 West Route 66. Well recommended and good for a westbound getaway in the morning.

For roadside eats, Miz Zip's Café at 2924 East Route 66 has been on the highway for decades. By all means check it out; just know that quality and service may vary. For dining in town, Josephine's Modern American Bistro at 503 North Humphreys Street has a well-deserved reputation. Fine service, excellent fare, and a super wine list. Down at 901 Milton Road, Bun Huggers features mesquite-grilled fare and burgers galore. If you're traveling with family, this would be the place.

Now, consider this. What would Flagstaff be like if it had become the motion-picture capital of the world? Because it almost was. A few years before Route 66 began service, a talented and extremely ambitious young man was steaming west on the Atchison, Topeka and Santa Fe one evening. Folded in his coat pocket was a new screenplay, and in his mind's eye he could see every detail of how it would be produced. Not in New York, but in the real West, with genuine cowboys and Indians, under open skies. Fed up with Long Island studios where no one knew a cactus from a tin can, the young man was certain from his readings of Zane Grey that Flagstaff would be the perfect location. The film he would make there would be grand, sweeping, magnificent—an epic.

It would also be wet—if he tried to make it in Flagstaff—where great, sodden flakes of winter snow were plopping softly into streams of icy mush along the platform as the train pulled in. For young Cecil B. DeMille, though, one look was enough. He never even left his Pullman but went

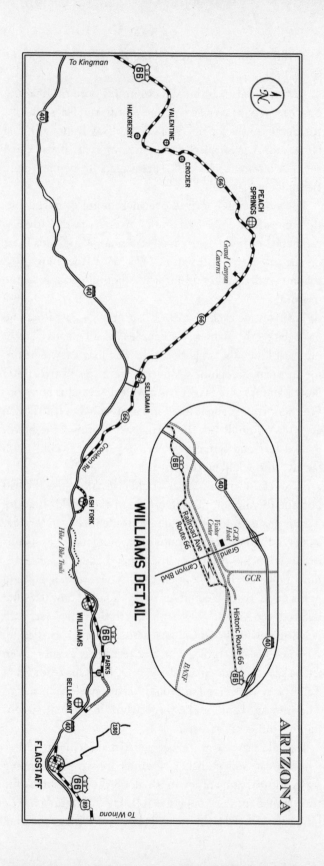

straight on through to Los Angeles, where he soon made the world's very first feature-length film, *Squaw Man* (1914), using drugstore cowboys from Sunset and Vine.

But the incident must have left its mark on him, for all through the monumental, biblical films DeMille later made, there always ran a theme of uncontrollable natural forces. To him that always meant water, lots and lots of water.

Which is how it came to be that today we can all enjoy Flagstaff . . . just as it is.

Flagstaff to Kingman

Beyond Business Loop 40, continue west on I-40. Near **Bellemont** you'll have a choice. Leave I-40 at Exit 185 to follow Brannigan Park Road, an optional 8-mile drive—over mixed gravel and pavement—leading to a stunning westbound section of paved old road.

Or continue west on I-40 and take Exit 178 north to CR 107, where a west turn onto that same pavement will take you through the village of **Parks** and along one of the most unspoiled sections of Route 66 anywhere. Until recently the roadbed remained unbroken 1930s concrete. Much of that has been blacktopped, but it doesn't change the feel of this segment, with the San Francisco Peaks behind and your future journey into vast western deserts still ahead.

At Deer Farm Road, rejoin the interstate. Business loops follow the old route through **Williams**. On the way into town, check your calendar. Arizona will celebrate its State Centennial in 2012. From that time forward, the Arizona State Railroad Museum, a major attraction will be open on a spectacular 16-acre site, complete with engine-house displays and locomotive exhibits, plus a special section devoted to Fred Harvey Company history. And with the Grand Canyon Railway based here in town, it's a perfect tie-in for travelers.

So make the Williams and Forest Service Visitor Center, at 200 West Railroad Avenue, your first stop for information on the town and its attractions. Close to town, several interesting trails have also been developed by the USDA Forest Service covering parts of old Route 66 now on the National Register. Hike-and-bikers will want to pick up a trails brochure and map. If the center is closed when you visit, look for trails between Exits 151 and 149 on I-40.

The Grand Canyon Railway, based here in Williams and making daily runs up to the South Rim of the Grand Canyon, offers a marvelous experience and is co-located with the Grand Canyon Railway Hotel, replicating the 1908 Fray Marcos Hotel, once a leading Fred Harvey property. This hotel earns top marks in virtually every category. Stay there if you can.

In town, the roughhouse period of Williams is carried by the Red Garter Bed and Bakery, located in a renovated 1897 bordello at 137 West Railroad Avenue, where a lady of whenever welcomes you from a window. For less carnal desires, Route 66 is well represented by Twisters 50's Soda Fountain at 417 East Route 66 Place. In short, Williams is the kind of town you just don't want to leave.

West of town, the long swing north of old Route 66 to Kingman begins at the Crookton Road Exit from I-40 west of **Ashfork**. Old, old roadbed is visible along this really wonderful stretch, and there's a special intimacy with the land here. **Seligman**, once a time-zone division point and now a home for goofy cars, is next. The Sno-Cap is a longtime Route 66 stop, as is Angel's Barber Shop—an early participant in Arizona's movement to preserve the old highway.

Farther along, on SR 66 to Kingman, you'll find Grand Canyon Caverns, one of the few attractions in the West to survive at such a distance from any interstate exit, due in part to thinking ahead. What to do with the empty land surrounding the place? An airport, of course, with two well-kept runways. Add a good restaurant, motel with Web access, and both transient and regional pilots are happy to fly in. You may even find aircraft parked among the cars. This is an interesting stop.

Now it's on to **Peach Springs** and **Crozier**, where the last unpaved section of Route 66 in Arizona remained until 1937. At **Valentine** you'll notice a brick schoolhouse on a hill to the north, dating from the days when the Bureau of Indian Affairs determined that children should be hauled—yes, in some cases kidnapped by private contractors—and forced to remain in schools like these. No further comment is needed; the school speaks for itself.

And if you think the ideals and style of the sixties in America are dead, you may find an exception in **Hackberry**. On the site an earlier general store, beneath classic Mobilgas and Greyhound signs, you may yet find a curiosity shop. Take time to visit a roadside story.

Kingman to Needles

Farther along, down a twenty-mile straight, **Kingman** comes into view. After sundown, it's like being on a long final approach—more like landing an aircraft than driving into town.

It's also worth noting that if the shadows are getting long, Kingman is within a day's drive of Los Angeles and the coast. And if you play your road cards right, you'll be inbound when several million people are outbound. Plus, you won't need to stay overnight in the low desert, where temperatures are hot as the dickens or close to freezing. Here on the high desert, Kingman has ample lodging in all price ranges.

Along Andy Devine Avenue, there are a few neon survivors like El Trovatore and the Brandin' Iron Motel, with a flickering sign that may read BRA IN. Farther down this winding stretch into town are some interesting retro-attractions, At 105 East Andy Devine is Mr. D'z Route 66 Diner. On the site of the old Triangle Cafe, this fifties-style eatery offers road-style food, a kitschy interior, and sidewalk seating so you can watch other Route 66 tourists on the highway watching you. Isn't it grand to be here first?

Another attraction is the Powerhouse Visitor Center at 120 West Route 66. This long-term restoration is the result of an extraordinary effort by a few volunteers that spilled over into the community, supporting a great save for a 1909 historic structure bypassed not by a highway, but by the construction of Boulder (now Hoover) Dam nearby. Demand crumpled, taking need for the old powerhouse with it. Yet Kingman found the wherewithal

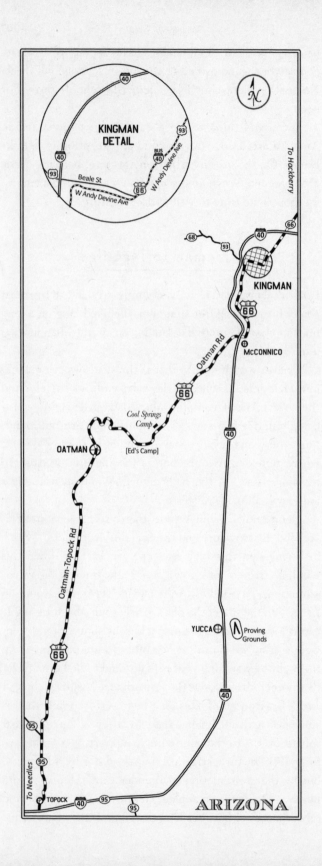

KINGMAN
DETAIL

Beale St

W Andy Devine Ave

W Andy Devine Ave

To Hackberry

KINGMAN

McCONNICO

Oatman Rd

Cool Springs
Camp

[Ed's Camp]

OATMAN

Oatman-Topock Rd

YUCCA

Proving
Grounds

To Needles

TOPOCK

ARIZONA

to bring back the structure from near ruin. The Power-house Gang did an amazing job. Stop in.

A classic Kingman highlight is Santa Fe steamer #3759 in downtown Locomotive Park, She's a huge Northern-type locomotive fast enough to haul passenger manifests through this unforgiving country. If you know only diesels on railroads, stand alongside this engine and look up. It helps with perspective.

Beyond Locomotive Park, watch for the sign: TO OAT-MAN. Bear left at the Y and continue on the old route through a deep cut to the **McConnico** undercrossing. At the stop, turn west under the interstate and follow the road through **Oatman**, the last and best part of the west-ern Arizona section of old Route 66. The time from Mc-Connico to Topock via Oatman will be a little over an hour, plus sightseeing. The I-40 route is about 45 min-utes, so the interstate doesn't save all that much.

Be forewarned, however. If you are a longtime flat-lander or are driving an RV that handles about like the Graf Zeppelin in a high wind, you may want to take the inter-state and continue your tour of old Route 66 in Needles. Otherwise, precautions noted, carry on.

If a major part of your driving time until now has been up on the superslab, you'll be surprised how quickly civili-zation fades once you are away from town. There are real beginnings and endings here on old Route 66, and a truer sense of being alone, dependent on your vehicle and the road itself to take you safely through. Along this stretch especially, there's often the very first glimmer of how it must have been for travelers forty or fifty years ago.

As you roll deeper into the desert, a more primitive part of the brain begins to stir. You may find yourself lis-tening more carefully to the engine, checking the gauges, feeling with your hands what's happening on the road just below. You may even hear some mechanical notes never audible to you before. Funny how perfectly good engines can sound rough way out here.

But before heading up Gold Hill Grade leading to Sitgreaves Pass, you'll discover the reincarnation of Cool Springs Camp as a gift shop and auto-art museum. Not long ago the stone-arched 1926 Mobilgas station was only a trashed ruin. Now with vintage gas pumps out front and a friendly welcome inside, the place captures your imagination. This is part of how it was; this is how it can be.

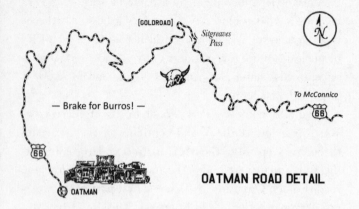

OATMAN ROAD DETAIL

Up to this point, where the grade begins in earnest, your main concern will be the odd jackrabbit or roadrunner grown unused to traffic. But you can soon expect other road companions. Wild burros, brought here by prospectors long ago and turned loose, now number in the thousands. They also blend so well into the desert scrub that it is difficult to see them before they saunter onto the road to inspect you. Protected by the Wild Horse Act, they are not timid. And if you pull over for a moment to take in the view, you may hear them calling to one another—perhaps announcing your arrival. For they are born tourist hustlers with an acquired taste for the junk food we are known to have with us.

This segment of old Route 66 is also just the ticket for drivers or riders with an affinity for switchbacks. And if you fancy yourself something of a canyon sweeper, the run over Sitgreaves Pass may be just what you've been waiting for.

Either way, imagine an alpine road dropped down into the middle of the American desert. Instead of black ice and maniacal Italian bus drivers, you'll be dealing with scattered patches of shoulder gravel, rockhounds in 4x4s, and the occasional band of wide-angle choppers. Still, the highway surface, curves, and gradients are a miniature version of the Stelvio run in the Italian Alps.

Back in the day, when cars and trucks had little power, even in first gear, the only way up the 3,500-foot grade east was in reverse—a craft mastered so well by locals that they could do it at top speed, by rearview mirror only, while draping one arm loosely out the window. So as you drive these marvelous old switchbacks, imagine how city-bred easterners must have felt when they veered into a blind, cliff-hanging curve, only to encounter some mad local coming full steam up the mountain backward. Commercial laundries at the bottom of the hill must have done a helluva a business.

Just over the Sitgreaves summit, you'll discover the earthly remains of **Goldroad**. A mini-boomtown once. Now just a few adobe walls and stone foundations, the owners having decided to save on their taxes by burning the town to the ground. So much for architectural and cultural heritage. And the tax code.

Once at the center of rich finds, this entire area had already been well picked over by prospectors when one José Jerez discovered a major new outcropping of gold. The town boomed again as everyone cashed in on the find. Everyone but José, that is, who spent his small share and then walked out by the road one night, sat down, and chugalugged a bottle of rat poison. *C'est la prospérité.*

On down in **Oatman** the main street is a curious jam-up of showboating, gun-toting locals and camera-laden tourists. Plus, of course, the omnipresent burros who, while happily hustling everybody, should be fed carrots only. Take a while to explore the character of this place that, booming or broke, has always gone its own way. Check out the shops for interesting art. And be sure to look in on the Oatman Hotel, best known as the honeymoon hideaway of Clark Gable and Carole Lombard. Town talent also puts on a floozie revue, alternating with staged gunfights, usually on weekends.

Heading west out of town, turn south at the Y toward **Topock**, where you'll rejoin I-40 westbound into California. Except for the pavement, this sobering desert section of old Route 66 has not changed since Dust Bowl days. If it's any time around summer, you'll know why the Joads walked out into the Colorado River shallows after driving this stretch and just stood there. In heat, the road from Oatman to Topock can be as tough as any road ever gets.

And at night, from the early 1930s until the mid-1950s,

this desolate section of road had everybody reaching for their car radios. Back in AM-radio days, you might have some trouble with static if a thunderstorm rolled in over the route. Otherwise, a broadcast signal wasn't limited to ninety miles or so, as FM is. Instead, AM reached out hundreds or—with a good skip—even thousands of miles to eager listeners. So as you rolled along the highway, network shows like *The Jack Benny Program* or *The Adventures of Sam Spade* could be tuned in virtually anywhere along old Route 66, even here in this empty desert. Still, back in the thirties and forties, you didn't worry so much about getting lost out here if *Amos 'n' Andy* were along with you.

Radio rode with you then, shortening the miles and bringing something both extraordinary and familiar to the solitude of a two-lane road through the desert, where even the rocks are burned black.

CALIFORNIA

Crossing into California isn't the adventure it once was. But neither is it the terror.

Back in the Dust Bowl days there were barricades out here on the road. Armed men too—local bullies mostly—many hired from the worst of the saloons along the highway. Men itching to call out anyone they didn't know, shoot anything that moved, club anyone who might resist. California was terrified, all right. Frightened silly that this stirred-up cloud of people would discover that they could be an army. An army that could take the whole state if it wanted. And right here, close to the border, is where that fear showed most.

A man with a Sam Browne belt and heavy, rib-kicking boots would be looking down the long ragged line of over-loaded, steaming jalopies. Peering into the first car. Studying some patient, fumbling man at the wheel, the enduring but crumpled face of his wife, and the sit-still-now looks of the children, their eyes shifting from the glinting badge to the black billy club now in momentary repose at the open side window.

You folks plannin' to cross? Stupid question. What would they be doing in line for near a day if they didn't intend to cross? But barricades and shotguns are the tools of men who are themselves desperate in some way. Intelligence is rarely deputized.

You folks got any money? Uh-huh. How much? Let me see it.

The money is produced. There isn't a lot, even by Okie standards, but it's something. A little change, a few sweat-soaked bills folded into a waistband pocket still stretched from the watch it no longer holds.

Avoiding the officer's all-seeing eyes, the driver sneaks a quick glance back over his shoulder at the family in the next car down the line, fearing that he is somehow holding them up.

The cop is looking more carefully at the kids now. Any sign of disease? Any excuse at all to turn the car back, send these people over some other border? But there is no reason. Thinking of his own family, perhaps, the man with the badge steps back and without expression waves the car on.

But before he is out of second gear, the freed driver can see in his mirror that the car behind has already been turned away and out of line. Sent back to Arizona or somewhere else. Sent to anywhere but here. For any reason. For no reason at all . . .

Things have changed since then, of course. Or have seemed to. The agricultural inspection station was even moved some years back. Crossing into California is no longer a problem unless you happen to be an inveterate apple snacker or cactus collector. And, thanks to equal opportunity, some of the agricultural inspectors are more than pleasant; they are lovely. A nice touch. A bit of Tinseltown way out here on the desert.

Few travelers think of the desert as being the real California, though. Not the California of laid-back surfers, iron-kneed skateboarders, and delectable beach bunnies. That California still lies well to the west. The desert here is a harsh, tough place. A place where the well-watered

California dream has not yet made its mark. The other California is closer to the sea, where life is easier, where both cars and humans seem to endure forever.

At a traditional picnic held in Los Angeles by emigrants from Iowa, some have been heard to say that California is a crazy place. Perhaps that's so. Perhaps all those people from Iowa are being held captive out here without anyone's knowledge. Perhaps, as someone also suggested, the continent has tilted so that everything not screwed tightly down comes sliding down into Southern California. If that's true, it has produced a wondrous blend.

So welcome to California. Spiritual home of the Sing-Along Messiah. Birth state of right-turn-on-red. It's an interesting place.

Needles to San Bernardino

Rejoin I-40 just south of **Topock**, where you'll notice a graceful silver-arched bridge over the Colorado River. It once carried old Route 66 and now serves as a pipeline support. A lesser job, perhaps, yet one allowing the span to remain as beautiful as ever.

Continue on the interstate to the exit for US 95 to the south that will lead you through an underpass and into **Needles**. Some desert travelers believe Needles was named for the prickly desert heat. Not true, though. The town was named for the spiky mountains to the south.

Notice also that from Needles west, there are over a hundred miles of open desert with few services before Barstow, so you may want to see to your vehicle's fluids and your own before heading up into the next range of mountains.

Broadway is a fairly direct route through town and is especially recommended in summer. For an optional route, closer to the original, bear right at the Y onto Front Street. You'll pass the once magnificent El Garces, formerly a grand Fred Harvey hotel, now on its way to full restoration. Keep a good thought.

After a turn and bend to the north onto North K Street, continue to a left turn on Walnut Street and a right onto

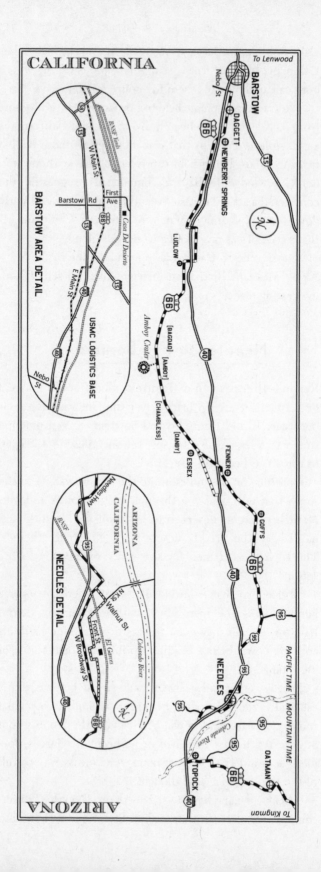

West Broadway Street / Needles Highway. Turn south-west and continue under I-40, following West Broadway Street / Needles Highway through a few bends until crossing over the interstate. After another bend on the north side, rejoin I-40 / US 95.

Beyond the Needles exit at US 95 for a forty-mile segment of the old route that ran through **Goffs** until 1931. An interesting, crusty desert town, Goffs is a survivor in its own right—one of those places that wouldn't know how to give up. Once, because it is usually at least fifteen degrees cooler than Needles, Goffs was a regular little summer resort. Now, even with air-conditioning common-place on the desert, the town carries on somehow.

To continue on the old route, cross under I-40 near **Fenner**. You'll be on a well-known section posted as National Old Trails, of which this highway was a part before becoming Route 66. Or if you've been following the interstate, take the **Essex** cutoff. From here, keep a lookout ahead. Just a few miles beyond the interstate exit, where the road curves down and away to the right, you'll get a first look at what lay in wait for the pioneer or the Dust Bowl family. Imagine the feeling: just when you have struggled up the terrible grade west of Needles and believe the worst to be over, you see what must yet be endured.

Out beyond the shimmering, glass-hard desert floor in front of you is another range of mountains, a thousand feet higher than those you just crossed. And beyond them yet another great barrier range, higher still. Peaks to 10,000 feet, some still carrying the snows of winter. Perhaps you tremble a little at the thought of what it will be like to go on. Most did tremble. And some, taking in the seeming endlessness of these trials, just stopped their creaking wagons or steaming old cars and without a word to anyone, walked away into the desert and disappeared. It was not a good end. But it was a way to have it over with, and that's all some could find for themselves in this merciless place. Just an end to it all.

On toward the remnants of **Danby** and **Chambless**, though, the desert takes on a different meaning. Seventy some years ago, the desert here meant not death but a chance at life. It was during World War II and a very bad time for America, just then. The brilliant General Erwin

Rommel, Hitler's Desert Fox, was loose with his Panzer Corps, racing almost unopposed across North Africa toward the unlimited supply of oil. If we could not support the beleaguered British there soon, and stop Rommel, the war would most certainly be lost.

Enter the singular General George S. Patton, "Old Blood and Guts" himself. Patton had been reared in this part of California and knew that the Mojave was not only similar to North Africa but sometimes worse! So Patton pressed every tank, truck, motorcycle, and reconnaissance aircraft he could into service as part of his Desert Training Center. Over two million men were trained to survive in the 10,000 square miles of desert surrounding you right now. In the end, the Great Mojave did its job. And Patton and the Second Corps did theirs, sweeping through North Africa as if they knew their way around—with no surprises their own desert hadn't already shown them.

The Great Mojave is quiet again now, a place for reflection. In abandoned **Amboy**, you might even reflect on buying the whole town; it may still be for sale. To the south, if you're a hiker and it is not summer, you may want to take a look into the Amboy Crater. Just take care with direction. You will not be able to see your car after you're out on the desert floor.

A few miles from Amboy lie the overgrown remains of Bagdad, inspiration for the film *Bagdad Cafe*, which you may want to stream or rent. Actually shot in Newberry Springs, the film is a marvelous tale of human relationships and the level of endurance and personal responsibility it takes to transform misgivings and self-pity into trust and love. As they do in real life, the road and the desert strip away all but the essentials. Old Route 66 offers a way in and a way out. Everyone is free to choose either direction, with the desert burning away everything else. You may enjoy the movie or, funny as it is, you may find it distressing. Either way, you'll not soon forget it—or this stretch of highway.

A break in the old road occurs at **Ludlow**, once a railcamp town and now just a high-priced fuel stop. To continue on Route 66, cross under I-40, head west over what may be a rough road, and then cross over the interstate at

Lavic Road for a short run to **Newberry Springs**. Re-cross to the north side of I-40 there, continue on to **Daggett**.

Now an aging bridesmaid among railroad towns, Daggett was once a major transshipment point for the borax trade from Calico to the north. Fat and sassy, Daggett developers learned that the Santa Fe Railway planned a major switching complex there. But the developers drove the price of land so high that the complex was built over at Waterman Junction instead. Later the new site was given the middle name of the railroad's president, William Barstow Strong. Downtown Daggett now has little more than the Desert Market and—if you're in luck and it hasn't disappeared by the time you get on the road—at least part of the Stone Hotel, once a favorite hangout for Death Valley Scotty, Tom Mix, and Wallace Beery.

Just west of Daggett, old Route 66 passes through a US Marine Corps Logistics Base gate—closed for the foreseeable future—so turn south at Nebo Street to rejoin the interstate into **Barstow**, exiting at Main Street. I-40 ends here, with I-15 continuing on to San Bernardino.

Route 66 continues on Main Street in town. For a look at one of the leading Santa Fe / Harvey House restorations, turn north on First Avenue, and after a bend east, Casa Del Desierto comes into full view. Acquisition and renovation of this marvelous property has been a long-term struggle for local volunteers, but their hard work is paying off. And like La Posada and others, this place will regain its glory.

Main Street in Barstow becomes Route 66 / National Old Trails, leading west through **Lenwood**, **Hodge**, **Helendale**, and **Oro Grande**. It's an easy drive of 38 miles or so on a well-maintained highway. Scenery is mixed: some high desert, some river basin.

That means you'll have plenty of time to speculate on roadside businesses like Honolulu Jim's that once populated this part of the route so long ago. How did the owner happen upon the name? Had he been a sailor stationed at Pearl Harbor? Or like others in the tourist business along old Route 66, was he simply a master marketer? Ah, Honolulu Jim's. How does it manage to sound so

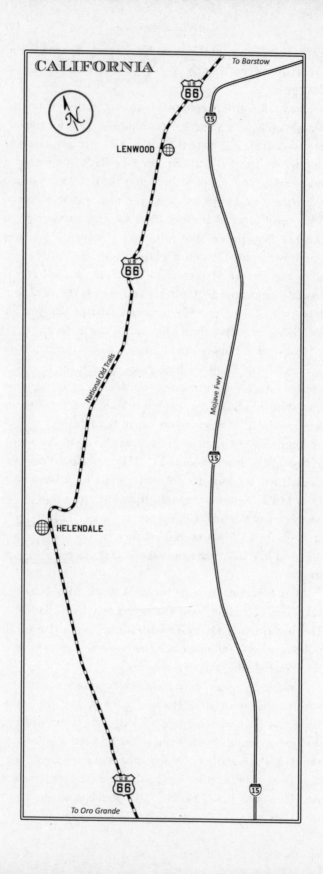

wholesome, yet still carry a slight tinge of something illicit? Who could resist stopping for a cold ice-cream soda, a chocolate malt, and perhaps a good lei?

The old route crosses under I-15 to enter **Victorville**, where D / Main Street to Seventh Street was the alignment through town. And while you're here, fuel up. Victorville's prices are probably better than you'll find for some time. From Victorville across the Cajon Pass nearly all the old route lies directly beneath the interstate.

Seventh Street merges into I-15 southwest of town and leads you out onto the high desert and over the last great mountain barrier to the West Coast. On reaching **Cajon Summit**, consider taking the Oak Hill exit for the old Summit Inn on Mariposa Road since 1952. This was a regular stop when topping the Cajon Pass and, if open, can still be a big deal. Try the cinnamon rolls with coffee. Look at the abandoned Route 66 roadbed, lean back, and imagine how it was—struggling up through the pass on the old road, or sailing down with tissue-paper brakes. Makes the coffee taste even better, doesn't it?

On the western slope, several sections of Route 66 still survive and are drivable. Beyond SR 138, take the exit for Cleghorn Road and continue on the west side of the interstate to the Kenwood Avenue entrance to I-15.

At **Devore**, you may take the exit to Cajon Boulevard that parallels I-215 and follow it to southbound Mt. Vernon Avenue. A more convenient route—unless it is morning rush hour—is to exit I-215 at 5th Street which flows right into Foothill Boulevard / SR 66 and the old route.

San Bernardino to Pasadena

A city in cultural transition, **San Bernardino** has often found itself trapped between two opposing views. On one side is the kind of thinking that led city officials to burn down a landmark Route 66 motel on Mt. Vernon Avenue just so the fire department could have some practice on a slow day. On the other side is a civic heritage movement which, among other projects, guided the restoration of the famous California Theater. Located at 562 West 4th Street, adjacent to the old route, the California was designed by

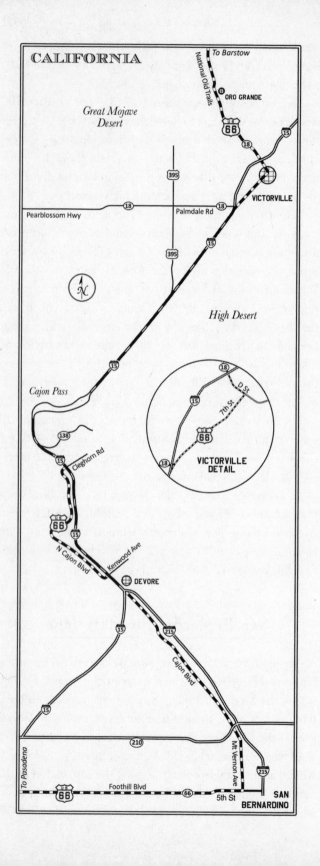

John Paxton Perrine and completed in 1928. Not far from the 5th Street exit, it's worth a look.

In those days, movie palaces commonly employed vaudeville acts to draw a larger audience, and the California was a major break-in theater for new talent. When sneak previews became common in the 1930s, the Santa Fe Railway became a virtual commuter line for all the stars who trekked out from Hollywood to San Bernardino to find glory or disaster in the first public showing of their latest films.

Will Rogers made his last public appearance at the California in 1935, headlining a benefit performance, featuring stars like of the day like Buster Crabbe and Jane Withers, to unknowns like Rita Cansino, who would be later recognized as Rita Hayworth. Less than two months later Will was gone, killed in a plane crash on Alaska's North Slope with his pilot and good friend Wiley Post. But the theater is still here, fully restored (now air conditioned, too) and rich with the original voice of its great Wurlitzer pipe organ. And thanks to local support, there may be a good show onstage. It's a grand place to breathe in a moment from Southern California's golden past.

Of course this is the present, and crossing L.A. on eighty miles of city streets can take more than a full day. Here are some suggestions from a former long-term resident—which would be me. Foremost, notice that Los Angeles proper is only one of several regions. It's been said that L.A. is a collection of suburbs in search of a city. That's still true.

So avoid driving *into* these subareas—Pasadena, Glendale, Hollywood, and Santa Monica, for example— between seven and ten in the morning. And avoid driving *out* from city centers from three to seven on weekday afternoons. The same is true for the freeways. There are lots of other things to do during these hours. Mondays aren't so bad. But Murphy's Law, with Dreaded Gridlock, rule supreme on Fridays. If you want an easy time on the freeways, Sunday morning is pretty good—everywhere but along the coast. Or if some 18-wheeler drops a load of eggs or pickles and maple syrup. It happens more often than you might imagine . . .

Take a careful look at the Los Angeles Metropolitan

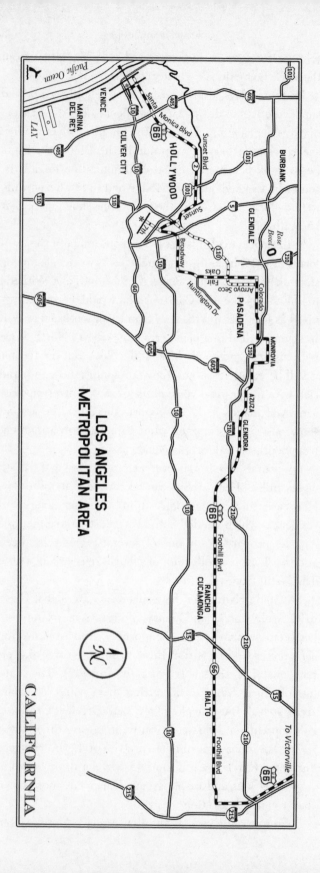

Area map. What you're really seeing on the page represents a total area of nearly 33,000 square miles. If you say that out loud, it has quite a ring to it. To save flipping back and forth, the entire area is shown on one page. If a jam-up occurs, you'll see your options quickly.

Note: If you are eager to complete your journey and simply want to reach ocean breezes in Santa Monica, jog south from Foothill Boulevard on I-15 and take I-10 all the way west. Once in Santa Monica, exit to Lincoln Boulevard—which was the official end of the route—turn north on Lincoln, then west again on Colorado, and continue to Ocean Avenue. This is now where the City of Santa Monica has declared Route 66 to end: right at the Pier. It's an easy route on the freeways and you can be there in a couple of hours if you plan your crossing during midday or evening. Go to page 128 to learn more about the end of your journey. Otherwise, carry on.

With a half day or more, there is a nice combination route to follow that will keep you on the old alignment most of the way with least difficulty. From San Bernardino, continue west along Foothill Boulevard / SR 66. Just east of Pepper Avenue in **Rialto** is the site of the twin to Holbrook's Wigwam Village. Restored and well-kept, this place has made a real comeback.

Although settlement of this region in Southern California stems directly from cultivation of the first orange groves and vineyards in the state, nearly all of that milk-and-honey life is gone, now replaced by a drive toward security rather than quality of life as the prime consideration. Huge lighted signs on outsize buildings along this stretch carry martial nouns like SENTINEL, FORTRESS, and GUARDIAN, which appear with the same frequency as the word *Acme* once did in Warner Bros. cartoons. Now and then a light, earthy noun like SPRINGTIME pops up. But not often.

If you've ever heard an old-time radio recording of the running Jack Benny gag about a train that went through "An-a-heim, Azu-za, and Coook-a-monga," you're in luck. **Rancho Cucamonga** is next along the route. This section of Foothill Boulevard was originally a Mormon farm-to-market road, hacked out of dense brush by settlers in 1852. Later, much of the area was given over to vineyards.

Look for the Virginia Dare Winery at Haven Avenue; it's one of California's oldest.

At Archibald Avenue, there's a Richfield Oil station built in the 1920s. And the Sycamore Inn—a very special place and once a San Bernardino Stage stop—has been offering good food and friendly service since 1848. If it's getting close on to suppertime, consider a stop. Just as interesting and inviting in its own curio style is the Magic Lamp—catty-corner across the street at 8189 Foothill Boulevard.

In **Upland**, at Euclid Avenue, a statue of Madonna of the Trail (no relation to the star-crossed singer) marks the end of National Old Trails and stands as a tribute to the pioneer women of the westering movement. Approaching **Glendora**, you'll have a choice of routes. For the older and more interesting 1930s alignment, turn north on Amelia Avenue and then west again on a somewhat displaced Foothill Boulevard. Some of these main-street buildings haven't changed in a hundred years, which is what the good people of Glendora intended. Jog south again on Citrus Avenue to rejoin Foothill Boulevard, and continue west.

At **Duarte**, you'll make a seamless transition onto East Huntington Drive. In **Monrovia**, jog north on Shamrock Avenue, then west again on Foothill Boulevard. Just beyond Myrtle Avenue, at 311 West Foothill Boulevard, you'll find the justly famous Aztec Hotel, designed by Robert Stacy-Judd in 1926 as an all-out tourist grabber for the new Route 66. It's now on the National Register and worth a stop whether you are on surface streets or taking the interstate. The patio is delightful and you'll half expect to find Sydney Greenstreet holding forth in the Elephant Bar and Restaurant.

Turn south on Santa Anita Avenue and continue west on Colorado Boulevard into **Pasadena**. You're now on the Rose Parade route, so you might not want to try this on New Year's Day—unless New Year's happens to fall on a Sunday. Why? Because this is genteel Pasadena, where in an age-old deal with local churches, the Tournament of Roses committee agreed never to do it on Sunday. Too immoral? No, parishioners were concerned that the parade might have frightened the horses tied up during services. Parade or no, take time for architectural and museum tours here if at all possible. Much can be found that is truly extraordinary.

From Colorado Boulevard, the alignments of old Route 66 divide. The newer alignment followed the 1941 Arroyo Seco Parkway and Pasadena Freeway SR 110 south to Sunset Boulevard. This route is shown as optional because the Arroyo Seco Parkway is almost always crowded, and with its right-angle on-ramps, can be dicey as well.

The preferred routing is an earlier version that turns south on Fair Oaks Avenue, following Huntington Drive and North Broadway into **Central Los Angeles**. Originally, Route 66 ended at 7th Street, but there's no need to go that far south. Instead, the route turns northwest on Sunset Boulevard / SR 2 and west on Santa Monica Boulevard. Though better known now as one of the main routes through Hollywood, this routing passed once-famous Ptomaine Tommy's restaurant, where the Chili Size was invented back during the Great Depression.

Along Sunset Boulevard in the Echo Park District, just a block south at 1100 Glendale Boulevard, is the famous Angelus Temple built by Aimee Semple McPherson in 1923. Probably no one soared to quite the evangelistic heights reached by Sister Aimee, whose charisma and career survived publicized divorces, a self-described kidnapping of epic proportions, and dozens of simultaneous lawsuits. Throughout the 1930s and '40s, the temple itself became a prime tourist attraction along old Route 66.

From Sunset Boulevard, follow SR 2 west onto Santa

Monica Boulevard. Above you, to the north, will be the famous HOLLYWOOD sign. Imported as a name from a Chicago suburb, the name was originally Hollywoodland, a real estate development west of Griffith Park. A landmark for motorists, pilots, and the starry-eyed, the sign has stood through thick and thin. With maintenance first discontinued in 1939, the sign has survived vandals, petty bureaucrats, destructive Santa Ana winds, and the stigma added by an actress's high dive from the top of the first letter to her death below. Now, with the LAND portion gone, the sign has been repaired and remains a beacon for a city that has officially never existed.

Continue west on Santa Monica Boulevard, through the boutique and little-theater district, past shops just on the trailing edge of trendy. In **Santa Monica**, 9th Street will be your heads-up for a turn south on Lincoln Boulevard.

A natural tendency is to want old Route 66 to extend from shore to shore. But it didn't truly begin at Lake Michigan and never officially ended at the Pacific Ocean. After being extended from Los Angeles to Santa Monica in 1935, Route 66 joined US 101A on Lincoln Boulevard southbound, ending at Olympic Boulevard. That was still the official terminus when Route 66 was decertified in California in 1963. Sadly, that intersection was fairly well trashed by the freeway offramp.

But Route 66 has always been a highway of fantasy as much as history, and on the November 11 anniversary of the highway in 2009, the Santa Monica Pier at Ocean Avenue, was designated—however unofficially—as the end of the trail for Route 66 travelers. Just north of the Lincoln Boulevard–Olympic Boulevard end-point, and a bit west on Colorado Avenue, the Santa Monica Pier makes a fine storybook ending. If you're a Redford and Newman fan, you'll want to take a ride on the beautifully restored carousel—it's the one used in George Roy Hill's classic film *The Sting*. The Santa Monica Pier is a Southern California tradition and full of curiosities. It's also as far west as you can go without getting wet.

To the north, across Ocean Avenue at the end of Santa Monica Boulevard, is a plaque memorializing Route 66 as Will Rogers Highway. Actually, the plaque was part of a promotion for the 1952 film *The Story of Will Rogers*. If

you're observant, you may even have noticed a highway marker announcing such in John Ford's production of *The Grapes of Wrath,* released in 1940. How do you suppose that happpend?

Close by the beach, the 3rd Street Promenade, between Santa Monica and Broadway Street, is worth a brief stroll, and at 1438 2nd Street, you'll find an extraordinary bit of history. The small brick building now appears to be the oldest structure in Santa Monica. It was constructed in 1873, became a saloon and, for a time, city hall. But the place is most remembered for being part of the Vitagraph Studio, when the company moved west from New York in 1911. A century later, Santa Monica is growing into the film and entertainment center it was perhaps always destined to be.

Before leaving this area, however, be sure to make a pilgrimage to Will Rogers's ranch, now preserved with the cooperation of the Rogers family as a California State Park. Drive northwest on Ocean Avenue three blocks, and at California Avenue, turn left and head down the hill to Pacific Coast Highway. Merge onto PCH northbound and continue a little over three miles, turn right onto Sunset Boulevard (yes, it's the same one), and wind inland to number 14253, on the left. Signs will guide you up to the ranch itself.

In this place, there's more of a feeling of Will himself—
what he loved and what enriched the caring he felt for all of
us—here on this lovely 185-acre spread than you'll find
anywhere else. Will's little office, where he did most of his
writing, is just upstairs. In the early morning, with wisps of
coastal fog hanging in the eucalyptus trees, you can practically feel the words coming through the window and down
into his old typewriter.

Wiley Post used to sideslip his new monoplane in from
the southeast, over the polo field, to land deftly on the
wide, sloping lawn next to the house. Bring a lunch—you
can picnic right on Wiley's runway. The whole place is
truly inspiring, and you'll enjoy just wandering about on
your own. In spring, when all the flowers bordering the old
board and batten ranch house are in bloom, it's a reminder
that paradise is not somewhere up, up, and away. It's right
here, all around. Some places just help us see it a little more
clearly. Will Roger's ranch is one of them.

Before going off to do any sightseeing, though, take time
to stroll along the boardwalk down on the beach or along
the winding path above the Palisades in Santa Monica.

We'll be parting company here, and it's a way of com-
pleting your journey over old Route 66 in a personal way.
Watch the people. Take in a sunset. Breathe some fresh
air before the city gets hold of it.

Like most travelers who come to Southern California,
you may not have exactly arrived. But the sea, the people,
and this place all let you know that you are here.

You are definitely here.

ROADSIDE
COMPANION

Over the decades, a few scenic highways—the Blue Ridge Parkway is one—have been built to celebrate and share the beauty of the lands through which they pass.

Route 66 is not one of those. Instead, its heritage reaches back to the Silk Road and earlier pathways of commerce. So Route 66 draws part of its beauty and mystique from the ingenious ways by which roadside merchants attracted travelers: something odd to see or photograph, an attractive facade, and light! One of the highway's well-deserved nicknames is the Neon Road. Just a night or two on Route 66 can make the point.

Yet, for those who linger along the roadside, it will be the stories that bring shape to memory. Not all the stories here bear the stamp of Absolute Truth; even a casual reading of the daily news will demonstrate that one person's science may be someone else's fairy tale. Just read and enjoy. Some Route 66 stories are rooted in a particular place or era. Others are timeless, born perhaps from the love that old road brings out in travelers.

The first of our three stories comes from composer Bobby Troup, now lost to us. His account of traveling Route 66 just after World War II is a classic in itself.

Writing "Route 66"

Oh, the memories . . . of Route 66 and that special time in America. I recall it all so well. Before World War II, my song "Daddy" was topping all the charts. In celebration I bought this olive green Buick convertible for myself and a black Buick sedan for my mother—I was buying everybody Buicks—and it was in that car that my first wife Cynthia and I started for California.

It was 1946 and I was fresh from a combat command in the Pacific with one of the first black Marine Corps units. I had decided to give myself one year in Hollywood to see if I could really make it as a songwriter.

The first day out we stopped at a Howard Johnson's near Pittsburgh. That was when Cynthia first suggested, quite hesitantly really, that I write a song about US 40. But there didn't seem to be any point to it because we were going to pick up US 66 soon. Cynthia laughed and said, "Get your kicks on Route 66." The phrase was so great that I began working on the song right away.

By the time we reached Chicago I had half the song written, and I'd measured the distance to L.A. on the map. It was over 2,000 miles. "Route 66" turned out to be one of the best songs I've written, though I didn't realize that at the time.

Many people know that part of the story by now, but what I've never talked about much was the trip itself. US 66 was known, of course, but it was usually called the Middle Route. It was strictly in the business of getting people to California—all the mystique of the road came later.

St. Louis, Missouri, was our first big stop. Louis Armstrong was playing a date at the Club Plantation over the first two weeks in February. I knew enough people in the big-band business from writing for Tommy Dorsey that we managed to get into a standing-room-only crowd. It was a great club, right on the original Route 66.

Not many new cars had come off the postwar assembly lines yet, so we had the road mostly to ourselves. That was just as well because a good part of the highway was absolutely miserable, narrow, just two lanes, and very twisting through the Ozarks and Kansas.

We stopped to see Meramec Caverns, of course. Everybody did. But in Texas our luck with the weather ran out when a blinding snowstorm blew down from the north. The wind was so bad that the snow was blowing horizontally across the road. It would be easy to get hit out there with trucks straying over the line, and there didn't seem to be any letup. The Buick convertible wasn't exactly weatherproof either, so we holed up in Amarillo.

Our car was running, all right, but the tires were badly worn and the engine was using a huge amount of oil. I was keeping track and it took seventy-five quarts in all before the trip was over.

I was really attached to that old Buick and it was hard for me to sell the thing. But the top was in tatters by then and the engine was beyond salvation. The last time I saw the car was on a weekly auction they once televised in Los

Angeles. A pitchman was saying that it had only been driven by a little old lady in Pasadena. But the crowd didn't believe him. There wasn't a single bid and they couldn't even get the poor Buick's engine to start.

We've all been through a lot since then, but it's wonderful to see the old road being preserved. I am indebted to the highway and all the road fans who love its music. Route 66 has been good to me and I feel honored to be part of a great revival.

When traveling, we tend to focus on the passing landscape and people we meet along the way. We seldom think of others on the road, often invisible to us—like bus drivers. This story comes to us from Howard Suttle, who in nearly thirty years as a driver for Greyhound covered over two and a half million miles across the Southwest, most on old Route 66. The story reminds us how much small things matter and that a mystery from the road often remains just that.

Missed Connections

One evening while en route from Albuquerque to Amarillo, we arrived at the Club Cafe in Santa Rosa for our evening meal stop. As passengers were unloading and going into the cafe, I noticed a slightly unkempt woman holding a small child, who was waiting to talk to me. I also noticed an old station wagon jacked up on the parking lot, as if it had broken down. The car was loaded with more kids and every conceivable household item that could be loaded, dragged, or tied on top. It reminded me that we don't have to go back to the thirties to see *The Grapes of Wrath*.

This poor lady, looking tired and dirty, managed a smile as she exclaimed, "Boy, am I glad to see you!" Asking her if she was going on the bus, she told me that they were en route to Gallup when the old car broke down. Their funds were depleted and it would take $200 to get the car going. It seemed the husband was moving them to Gallup and he was sending them a credit card on the bus so they could get the car fixed up and continue on their trip. The husband told her to meet this schedule to get the credit card.

After checking the baggage manifest, I found no shipment or package for Santa Rosa. The poor lady was very disappointed, for they had been there in that old car for hours. Unloading the baggage bins, I looked for what had to be a rather small package, but found nothing. Feeling really sorry for her, I could do nothing about it. While inside eating I mentioned her predicament to Phil, the owner, and he said that before going home after closing, he would make sure that they had something to eat.

After arriving in Amarillo around midnight, while clearing my belongings off the dash of the bus, I moved an old shop rag that had been thrown there by the previous driver. Lo and behold, there in a flat envelope was the credit card for those poor people. Obviously the driver who picked it up in Gallup had the intention of keeping it on the dash so I would see it, but while the bus was being serviced in Albuquerque, the cleaning boy threw it farther behind the instrument panel and the rag had covered it up. I felt that, just like any bureaucracy, we had been so busy with our own little problems that we had couldn't even deliver a small envelope. Now, *that* was efficiency.

The 12:30 A.M. schedule bound for Santa Rosa and Albuquerque was almost loaded. Taking the envelope to the driver, I asked him to please deliver it to that family. He would arrive in Santa Rosa about 3:00 A.M., which would be earlier than the mechanic could open his shop, so it would be the same as if I had delivered it. If Phil had given them food, I guessed it wasn't too bad after all.

The next evening I noticed the old car was gone, and I wished them the best. I remembered her smiling face as she approached me expecting that small package. I wondered how far they got.

This next story is from personal experience along the old highway one lonely night. It concerns nothing less than Texas chili and the effect it can sometimes have on folks.

From *Greyhound Tales from Route 66* by Howard Suttle. Coda Publications (2004). Reprinted here by permission.

A Bowl of Red

The café was situated in a scruffy, dying town—the name of which has conveniently escaped me—back when Route 66 was defunct after her signs were taken down. Still, I'd been told that this was a place where you could get the best chili anywhere west of Chicago.

Who could turn down a recommendation like that? At the time, though, it seemed more like a challenge. Even at the end of a long day, when sleep seemed more important than food, I had to find the place. It wasn't too difficult. The café—an old-fashioned chili parlor, really—was the only place along the main drag that had a lighted sign and was still open. After years of experience at driving through darkened towns, I nailed it on the third pass.

There's a saying about road writers: our main job is to get ourselves lost to save others the trouble. Anyway, I pulled into the small gravel lot and switched off the ignition.

The building must have been a house at one time and still showed its past, despite a walled-in front porch. Up three front steps and through a screen door with a twangy old spring, and I was in a tiny restaurant. A half-dozen stools lined a worn Formica counter, with empty tables scattered about in some random order. Add a drooping roll of flypaper and it could have been a movie set where Cagney or Bogart would have seemed right at home. I took a counter seat nearest the door, perhaps looking for an easy escape if this didn't go as promised.

The counterman or owner, I couldn't tell which, handed over a celluloid-covered menu. What a selection: chili of almost every persuasion. I played it safe and ordered from the center of the menu, avoiding the Alamo Survivor entry at the top, along with the one listed for Eastern Sissy down at the bottom. From the first spoonful, the chili was hot enough, all right. Woo-hoo! But still, oh so good . . .

One stool over sat a creased and weathered cowboy of some years, on whose cheeks you could have sharpened a chain saw. Yet even as he wolfed down his bowl of red, the man was weeping.

"Are you okay there, pardner?" I asked.

He looked at me and snuffed back to clear his nose. "Hell, no, I ain't okay. This here is really fierce."

"Then, if you don't mind my asking, why do you go on eating it?"

"Because if the stuff don't hurt some and turn you silly, it ain't no damn good."

"You ever been in love?" I asked.

"Yep," he said. "It's pretty much like this bowl of red here."

I've studied the human condition at some length and have yet to improve on what that cowboy said. His lesson was clear: Keep on going until you see the bottom of your bowl. You have a whole lifetime to nurture regret. But you can never make up for what you didn't try.

Enjoy the moment!

ILLINOIS

Highway-building has always been high on any list of priorities for Illinois. But the push for better roads sometimes came less from auto clubs and engineers than from Gangland, USA. With Prohibition in full swing, the likes of Hymie Weiss, Bugs Moran, and Al Capone needed high-speed roadways from Chicago south.

Illegal booze was being collected from neighborhood stills, hijacked from government warehouses, or brought in by speedboat from Canada. And like a bathtub drain, the booze was backing up. The Capone gang, in particular, needed to get their supplies moving.

The power of the gangs during the 1920s was enormous, reaching into every part of society. Today, when drug-running is diffused like an underground cottage industry, the concentration of that power is incomprehensible. But at the height of Capone's career there was no public office, from Chicago's city hall to the capital at Springfield, that he didn't control or influence.

At the time, Capone was paying $30 million a year in pretax, preinflation dollars to the police alone. So if Big Al wanted a fine new highway to St. Louis for his trucks and armed caravans, there sure as hell was going to be one. And why not make it a bright new US highway as well?

Route US 66 filled the bill, and not surprisingly, the necessary appropriations sailed through the Illinois legislature in record time. Concrete was going down almost before the ink was dry, and the rum-runners' convoys were soon rolling to mob distribution centers in St. Louis.

In downstate Illinois, ballrooms, barrooms, and bawdy houses all came under the control of Capone and his confederates. One of the most profitable was the Riviera (aka the Hideaway) near Gardner on Route 66, and Capone is said to have kept a place on the Kankakee River at Wilmington for his wilder parties—featuring whatever you can imagine, and probably more. If something was illegal, you could bet the crime lord bought it, sold it, or used it.

Capone had an unusual liking for pastel suits with matching ties and surrounded himself with equally colorful bodyguards. So when the boys climbed into their speedy Jewetts to accompany Big Al's armor-plated Cadillac on the new Route 66, it looked like rainbow sherbet rolling into town. Still, it was all a deadly business.

The first car was fitted with a cast-iron bumper meant to ram any misguided police flivver, while Capone's Caddy was safely tucked in the middle. The final car bristled with Tommy-gun men as a rear guard—all dressed in shades of yellow, mauve, sea green, and peach. Not that anyone laughed.

A frequent stop along Route 66 for Capone's entourage was one of the Rossi family businesses around Braidwood. As it happened, the eldest Rossi operated a saloon and grocery store, in addition to several dance halls in which the gang was interested. But what was most intriguing to the mobsters was the way in which Rossi kept his workers in line. Theft and double-dealing in the ranks was always a problem for Capone and the other bosses, so they were impressed by innovative thinking. After all, good gangies were too useful to shoot because of minor infractions.

One story the mobsters were sure to have heard concerned the loss of bottles from a private stock of homemade wine that the senior Rossi kept handy for "medicinal purposes." After weeks of trying to discover the culprit, he simply laced a few bottles with a powerful Italian laxative and waited. The next day, when one of his drivers couldn't stay out of the bathroom for more than a few minutes, Rossi pitched the thief out on his ear.

The mob certainly could have used that kind of talent. But even though the Rossis' dance halls mysteriously burned a short time later, the gang was never able to recruit any of the family and had to be content, as we are, with the story.

Farther south on Route 66, however, the gang gave the folks at Funks Grove an uneasy time. In the maple-syrup business since 1891, the Funk family is still known nationwide for the quality of their "sirup," and the entire supply normally sells out before summer each year.

Now, life in the sugar bush is pastoral and no one in Funks Grove had ever come in contact with the mob. The Funks only knew, as did everyone else in Illinois, that mere mention of Capone's movements could bring immediate death or worse. Fortunately, the mobsters usually rolled at night and on the sly.

What the Funks didn't know was that, in addition to colorful garments, Scarface Capone also had a whopper of a sweet tooth. It would have explained the slow file of heavy automobiles the Funks saw winding ponderously up the drive toward their sap house.

Once stopped, pastels appeared everywhere and a gunsel from the lead car ordered several cases of super-sweet maple syrup. The purchase made and loaded, a large man in yellow suit and matching fedora signaled with his cigar from the middle car, and the cortege wound slowly back out to the highway to head north.

The elder Funks looked at one another and decided on the spot that there was no one in any of the cars that they could ever recognize. In fact, maybe the line of cars hadn't been there at all . . .

A good decision for syrup lovers everywhere.

After Capone was sent to prison and the Great Depression began, his empire quickly came apart. Benedict's Standard Station in McLean noticed a drop in the quality of hoodlums stopping for gas. The molls, with their bee-stung lips and plucked eyebrows, looked shabbier in cloth coats instead of furs, and the men often wore unpressed, threadbare suits without ties.

For a time they tried valiantly to shake down the station

owner. But the eldest Benedict, a hickory-tough Kentuckian, would have none of it. He had no use for freelancers especially, since they were often less predictable, more dangerous. So he met them at the door with a double-barreled twelve-gauge. The station was vandalized now and again, but the gunsels soon gave up.

From then on, the Benedicts recall that the class of travelers along Route 66 through downstate Illinois took a turn for the better. Glenn Miller passed through, always the gentleman. So did Cole Porter, in a very stylish linen suit, driving a Jaguar 140 with professional aplomb. Elvis stopped by in later years, looking boyish and a little disconnected.

Shortly after that, sections of the new interstate highway began opening. The small towns of downstate Illinois were no longer in the mainstream. And all too soon, Route 66 began to disappear.

MISSOURI

Few places along old Route 66 offer so grand an entrance for the traveler as St. Louis. It's like approaching a citadel, with the Mississippi River as a moat—and the Chain of Rocks Bridge to cross over. Even the city's water intake towers, just south of the bridge, are built in the style of medieval castles.

Chain of Rocks Bridge was completed in 1929, just in time for the Great Depression, amid rumors, legends, and myths that persist to this day. Recent tragedies have only added to the stories. Flowers mysteriously appeared on the anniversary of a workman's death in a fall from the main span. Military aircraft being ferried to the East Coast for tests got stuck at the bend. And the bend itself is fascinating. Few bridges change course in midstream. Yet Chain of Rocks does. Why?

Some of the myths, now put to rest, suggest that the 24-degree bend was an afterthought or the result of a threat to the closest water-intake tower, or that a squabble over property rights left the bridge no place to land on the Missouri side. Another rumor was that the engineers failed to find sufficient bedrock for their creation.

All untrue. Instead, it appears that the bridge, if constructed in a straight line, would have presented a threat to safe navigation of the river where currents were strong and tricky. So the Army Corps of Engineers recommended the bend; it was incorporated in the original plans and specifications, and you can see for yourself that it worked out all right.

But for promoters, the bridge was not a good investment. Even without the Depression, a toll bridge that offered no direct route through or around St. Louis was doomed. The enterprise went broke and was refinanced at a loss of more than a million dollars. Yet the graceful structure and its tree-lined approaches somehow went on to capture the fancy of Route 66 travelers. The Chain of Rocks Bridge remains a favorite. Today you can even hike and bike across the bridge over a new trail.

Southwest of St. Louis, Route 66 runs through Ozark country, among the richest in scenery to be found anywhere. Each spring when the dogwood is in flower, the story goes, St. Peter has to lock heaven's gates to keep Ozark souls from returning home to a greater beauty.

By contrast, some homesteads along this same stretch are also among the poorest to be found anywhere. All of which makes the Great Jumbo Shrimp Disaster an event they still talk about from Rolla to Joplin.

Just east of the Hooker Cut, not far from Devils Elbow, the old highway twists along the edge of a steep ravine. And not long ago, a big tractor-trailer rig loaded with over 40,000 pounds of frozen Gulf shrimp overshot a tight bend in the road.

Slithering and crashing down the steep side of the ravine, the rig finally hit bottom with a bang that brought out just about everyone in the territory. Good thing, too, for the trailer caught fire and it was only by quick action and a half mile of garden hose that a handful of volunteers managed to put it out.

After a brief survey of the wreck, the locals realized the truck was going to be down there for quite a spell—and they began to think about what it would be like to have tons of burnt, rotting fish for a neighbor. So they began discussing ways to get the mess cleaned up and out of there. It was about then that someone discovered that if you knocked the outer layer of burned shrimp off each block of ice, the rest was still frozen solid.

A lightbulb appeared over the head of every mountain

man simultaneously. And in less than an hour, the trail up from the wreck looked as though it had been taken over by a colony of ants. Men struggled up the hillside to deposit their treasure boxes in the backs of pickup trucks. As filled trucks pulled away, more came to take their places. A makeshift road was eventually cut to reach the ravaged truck, and after that the loading went even faster.

By morning the battered trailer lay empty. Of course, in the early 1950s, not many of the folks in this region owned freezers, and few had ever tasted shrimp in any form. But the race was on to beat the thawing process.

Soon every family table featured fried shrimp, stewed shrimp, shrimp cocktail, and a kind of shrimpy Waldorf salad. Some, it is said, even tried shrimp pancakes and shrimp fritters. In the end, fishermen were even baiting their trout hooks with the stuff just to finish off the sorry mess.

The shrimp-truck disaster, everything considered, served up a hillbilly feast to beat all.

The devil figures prominently in many stories from the Ozark region, and Route 66 is no exception. Devils Elbow has been known for years as a lovely but difficult stretch of the old highway east of Hooker. Unfortunately, Devils Elbow is a term that refers not so much to the highway as to the river below.

Back in the 1800s, when rivermen brought timber and goods down the Big Piney River, they got pretty good at the job. With strings of log rafts nearly a mile long and a man in back with a stout snub-pole, they could negotiate every bend in the river with ease. Well, they could until the devil tossed a boulder off a cliff and down into the river—right in the middle of the river's sharpest bend.

When the Big Piney was running full, the devil's new obstacle posed no problem; the boatmen rounded the bend slick as could be. But when the waters were down, the blamed rock would tear up a whole string of rafts, ruining any chance of profit, and generally put the fear of God and dark angels back into everyone.

So if you drive along this section someday, it's best to remember that Route 66 is up on the rib cage somewhere.

Devils Elbow is down on the Big Piney where it's always been.

Attention, Elvis fans! If you're a true believer and expect the King to show up any day, you may be looking in all the wrong places. Most anyone in these parts will tell you so, because near the peak of his popularity, Elvis played the Shrine Mosque in Springfield. And it's the place to watch.

Probably the best promoted of all the entertainment facilities along old Route 66, the 4,000-seat mosque evolved from a home for Abou Ben Adhem Temple to a major stop for opera and dance companies, swing bands, and politicians. Just about every imaginable act was booked here at one time or another, from Spike Jones and his City Slickers to Archduke Felix of Austria.

But other than the night that Missouri-born Harry Truman appeared here in 1952, the hottest booking of all time was old swivel hips himself. Elvis rolled into town aboard a two-story bus, with his entire band, road crew, and personal attendants of every kind. But he was not happy. After that, accounts differ.

Some say box-office figures were not as promised; others suggest that there was a kink in some relationship of the moment. But everyone agrees that Elvis was thoroughly annoyed and his performance showed it. With barely a courtesy encore, the King let it be known that he hated, hated, hated Springfield and sure as hell wouldn't play this burg again. Bubba.

Springfielders didn't exactly mourn on their side either. The Elvis caravan rolled out on Route 66 and the matter was largely forgotten—except by one picker in the band who wouldn't let it rest. When a new facility was built in Springfield, he went to work on his boss. For months, the band member soft-soaped Presley. At long last the picker, who'd lived in Springfield and couldn't stand to hear the town taking continued abuse, resorted to pure begging. Aw, please. You'll love it. Trust me. Just give Springfield another chance. That sort of thing.

Elvis probably had all of that he could stand; he either had to let a good sideman go or play Springfield again. The King caved in. A date was scheduled at the new venue, and once again Elvis and company hit town. This time everything went swimmingly. Elvis was happy. The band and road crew were happy, and everyone present knew that the night had been a roaring success.

At the close of the performance an almost tearful Elvis promised—promised—that no matter what, he'd come back to Springfield. So this is the place to watch. Because you know, whatever else is said about the King, he always kept his word.

KANSAS

Americans are quick to throw out anything older than the family dog—and roads are no exception. Once Route 66 was decertified as a US highway, nothing protected it as a national treasure. One structure consigned to the wrecker's ball was the very last of the rainbow-style bridges built in the Riverton area. A main bridge and another span had already fallen to progress.

Sometimes called Graffiti Bridge, it found use as a kind of concrete bulletin board announcing who might be doing what with whom. During the American Bicentennial, in fact, the whole thing was painted red, white, and blue—possibly by local girls who were tired of seeing their names displayed there.

Yet regardless of pleas from the community, the span was scheduled for demolition. Government officials were committed to building a new bridge. The reason given was that the old structure didn't meet federal standards—not that it mattered, since the route was no longer a federal highway anyhow. In short, someone had decided there would damn well be a new bridge and that was that. The old one would have to come down.

Undaunted, the Kansas Historical Route 66 Association went on searching for a way to stop the destruction, and in the federal regulations, found a way to do it. Right there in official black and white, the regulations stated that when a new span is to be constructed, the old bridge need not be destroyed. It could be closed or even left open for limited traffic.

Caught short by regulations they'd not read, local officials agreed to spare the bridge, a happy ending for all who know that grand old bridges, like the highway itself, are best appreciated when employed as they were intended.

Kansas and Route 66 have clung to each other since the highway was commissioned. Part of that is due to the fact that Kansas was dry for a long time and state officials were tough about it. In recent years, before state prohibition finally gave way, Kansas went to court to stop airlines from serving liquor over its airspace. The state lost.

But back in the harshest of the dry days, bootleggers gained a powerful hold in this little corner of Kansas because when escape was needed there were two getaway states close by. Agents could rarely close in before the bootleggers were warned by an elaborate system of lookouts and alarms. Worse for the lawmen, many stills were completely portable.

On one occasion—with only a few minutes' warning—there was only time for the alky cookers to dump everything and make a run for it. All their brew, mash, and stills went off Ryan's Bridge into the river below in one huge illegal splash.

No one was arrested, since all the evidence had disappeared. Yet everyone in this part of the country knew where the stuff had been dumped. For as it happened, a flock of migrating geese were just downstream from the dumping. In an hour, they had taken on so much sour-mash cocktail that their flying ability dropped to near zero.

As a consequence, the geese made it only a little farther south. There, on the Route 66 bridge into Riverton, the whole flock of them—now absolutely plastered—ambled, honked, and staggered all over the bridge. The structure was narrow even for its day and vehicles had no room whatsoever to maneuver around the comical but now highly aggressive geese.

As their heads cleared, the geese took to the skies again.

And though their formation was ragged, the geese remembered Kansas as a place to have a good time. In subsequent years, the flock returned time and again to the waters below Ryan's Bridge—hoping, it would appear, for another free happy hour.

OKLAHOMA

You never knew what might be lurking just out of sight along Oklahoma's old two-lanes. Holdups were commonplace, and along some stretches, Route 66 was known as Robbers Road. Up around Commerce, though, life is more gently lived. The town is presently remembered as Mickey Mantle's birthplace. But it was almost known as Bonnie and Clyde's deathplace.

At the height of their unholy reign as America's most wanted couple, Bonnie Parker and Clyde Barrow pulled a hasty job northeast of here. And their getaway road was good old Route 66—best highway west to anywhere.

The usual scenario was that Bonnie and Clyde would roll in, rob a bank or shoot up some one-cop town just for the sheer hell of it, and then go busting down the road with the law lagging far behind. This time, though, the lawmen employed a brand-new weapon in their war against crime: the telephone. Quick as sound, the cops could call ahead, flashing the word to Oklahoma: *Stop 'em, boys. They're headed your way.*

It would take a little time to prepare, but Commerce was the best place to set up an ambush for the two lawbreakers. The advantage lay in two opposing ninety-degree turns in Route 66 the highway approaches Commerce from the east. Even in their quick Ford V8, Bonnie and Clyde would be slowed almost to a walk, and the lawmen would have the drop on 'em. Trouble was, not much firepower was available in sleepy Ottawa County. So the US military was called in.

The American government is always declaring war on something, too often with Custeresque results. Liberals lost their war on poverty and conservatives have certainly blown the war on drugs. Still, lessons seem to come hard to government types. So the war on Bonnie and Clyde was declared right there in Commerce. The army showed up with a heavy-caliber machine gun and its best gunners. A sandbag emplacement was readied in jiffy-quick time, and everyone scrunched down to wait. And wait.

Bonnie and Clyde had apparently stopped somewhere, raising a doubt about whether they would show up at all. What if they took some side road? *Good God, they could be in Arkansas by now.*

Moments later, a car was spotted tearing in from the neighboring town of Quapaw. Confirmation came quickly—it was definitely Bonnie and Clyde. The machine-gun crew was given the word to shoot the car to pieces and blow 'em away.

Angle and elevation were perfect as the lawbreakers' car skittered around the first turn on two wheels. *Steady now. Wait 'til they slow for the second turn.* Safety off, the gunners traversed their target, waiting for the order. Then it came . . . *FIRE!* A click was heard . . . and nothing else. The gun had jammed. Bonnie and Clyde, now seeing the ambush that had been in store for them, smiled sweetly and waved to all assembled. They tore on through town, throttle wide open, heading for Texas on Route 66.

And this time no one phoned ahead.

Having regularly endured drought, flood, and famine Oklahomans would at some point in the future be called upon to face pestilence as well. And sure enough, in the early 1940s, swarms of crickets moved in on Bristow. In a few days absolutely everything was covered with them: screens, doors, plants, and fences. They came down chimneys and turned up in garden hoses. People swept them off the sidewalk almost hourly to allow customers to get to businesses without tromping through insect stew. All to no avail.

For a while, the popular Hamburger King restaurant persevered. They swept the place clean each morning—and hourly thereafter—while clearing crickets from pantries and grills. Still, the tide of battle favored the crickets.

One morning a new addition went up under the sign that had always advertised the restaurant's World Famous Hamburger. Foreshadowing truth-in-advertising laws yet to come, it simply read: Cricketburgers.

A bit farther west, under the giant YUKON mill sign, Oklahoma's tradition of fair play in the face of the unexpected has always been most evident. The Yukon High School football team of 1943 was one of only two teams in the entire state that no other team had scored on over an entire season. Yukon also had a winning streak of thirty-four games in a row. So the folks in town knew how to bring up and support a team. But it is not a tradition easily won.

Even before US 66 was routed through town, Yukon was working on fundamentals. In the early days, the school had neither the equipment nor the money needed for a football program. So the merchants coughed up a hundred bucks for the team. The problem was that the money could buy pants or helmets but not both. Well, the team couldn't very well play in their skivvies, so the hundred bucks went for pants and the boys played bareheaded.

Real football shoes were a problem, too. But most players were able to make up for that by driving huge nails through their work shoes and playing barefoot during practice to avoid injuring their teammates.

The team's first game, with Geary High School, also on Route 66 for a time, was a tough one. Shoulder pads were nonexistent or were made up of old horse collars. Still, everything was going fairly well until a Yukon team member caught the ball, headed across the open field for the goal line—and disappeared.

For a moment the tiny crowd was stunned. Everyone raced for the point at which the player was last seen and found him stuck halfway down an open well that no one had noticed. He was pulled out safely by a team of horses, but a serious question remained about how to judge the action.

Some wanted to give the boy an automatic touchdown for his trouble. Others argued that he didn't deserve it since he'd been pulled out without being hurt all that badly. Still others insisted that the play be run over again. After some heated discussion, the Yukon team was awarded half the distance to the goal line and next down. Everyone except the boy, who'd lost his shoes in the fall, was satisfied.

Of course the gods of football still hang out in Oklahoma, so they must still enjoy the memory of that long-ago game between Yukon and Geary along old Route 66.

People in other states complain about the weather. Oklahomans collect it. And sometimes conditions were more than highway departments could deal with. So an experiment was tried while paving US 66 through Missouri and Oklahoma.

Quarter-round concrete lip curbs were poured on either side of the roadway's main slab. It was hoped that the curbs would prevent erosion during hard rains. Highway engineers also said that the curbs would help direct wayward cars away from a dangerous soft shoulder.

The idea sounded reasonable, but in the dipsy-doodle sections near Weatherford, everything went wrong that could. During a hard rain, the curbs directed so much water onto the highway that the hilly sections looked like giant sluice boxes. And when the temperature dropped after a hard rain from the north, each paved hill turned into something like a vertical ice rink.

Truck drivers knew the roller-coaster road quite well, of course. But fearing they would lose traction near the top of a hill if their speed dropped too much, they went hell for breakfast down each grade.

A well-known clergyman was known for doing the same thing while on missions of spiritual importance, since he felt divinity close at hand. A field engineer for the Oklahoma Highway Department recalls one frozen night when the clergyman and one of the wildest of the local truckers met.

Both the truck and the cleric's speeding flivver turned turtle on the spot—spreading, in quick succession, several hundred crates of frozen turnips and a Catholic priest across the icy highway.

No one was badly hurt and the priest returned to his parish house on foot to give serious thanksgiving. The road crew got back to work after doing their own amens. The turnips apparently passed right on to veggie heaven.

Despite the trials of the Dust Bowl years, simple human kindness was still in great supply. By contrast, our own recent recessions (no politician dares use the word depression today) have set new standards in meanness of spirit.

Yet back in the early 1930s, it was common for merchants to go all out for their customers during hard times. One Oklahoma native, now a retired school administrator, recalls that his father always carried the tenant cotton farmers who were his customers.

In 1929, those farmers were devastated when the price of cotton dropped to ten cents a pound. None of them could pay even a dime on their accounts. But the store owner was determined to see them through this one bad year. He sold off his own property, mortgaged the rest, and stayed in business. And at least a few farmers stayed on the land.

TEXAS

Some government officials—a few cops in particular—seem to have a way of overstepping their limits while pretending to serve the people. That's a common occurrence in big coastal cities, but it also happened at a famous nightspot in Amarillo back in the 1950s. The Nat—a natatorium that was later boarded over to become a ballroom—drew many of the top bands and performers after reopening in 1926.

Just a few doors from Route 66, the Nat was perfectly located for one-night stands by all the great names touring the country. Paul Whiteman, Benny Goodman, and Harry James all played here. But by the mid-1950s, big bands were out. It cost too much to keep them on the road, and except for the college-prom circuit, most disappeared from sight. Helping them into early retirement were the new solo acts with small groups of three or four sidemen. Rock and roll was hot, country and western was on the move—and the music was cheap.

Buddy Holly could be had for not much more than room and board and Willie Nelson was still working honky-tonks while he wrote great songs for other performers that producers would not let him record. Even the King was working the small rooms and out-of-the-way places. Of course that didn't last long, and eventually audiences would pay more for a single rock group than for a dozen swing bands.

That's about the time Little Richard was booked into the Nat. As soon as word got around, threats began to filter into the owner—not from offended citizens, but from law-enforcement officials, people charged with knowing better. The Nat's owner wouldn't stand for intimidation, however, and stated flatly that Little Richard would go on as planned.

The sticking point was the posturing that the performer was known to do onstage. Lewd and lascivious conduct, the sheriff said it was. Everybody else said it was great. Most thought nothing of the threat of arrest. Just smokeys blowin' smoke. Elvis Presley's act was far more suggestive, and it was hard to top (or even classify) what Jerry Lee Lewis did onstage. About all anyone could say is that he ended his shows with most of his clothes still on, even if he sometimes burned the piano. By comparison, Little Richard might not be a garden-club act, but he was well within accepted limits for the High Plains.

The real trouble, of course, was that Little Richard was African American. And that was what really got him busted that night at the Nat. Roughed up and hauled away in cuffs before doing anything, the performer was slapped with a stiff fine and escorted to the city limits. Today the story is still told to Route 66 travelers. That's a good way, people here believe, to keep present lawmen on notice that it would be better if something like this did not happen again.

Some men naturally combine business ability and showmanship. Far fewer men also possess the air of gentle toughness it takes to create something of great value for the community, in spite of hard times. Cal Farley was one of those few.

A wrestling champion and semipro baseball player, Cal always seemed to be in the thick of things. Soon after the Amarillo Gassers folded as a baseball team, he took over a failing tire shop and established one of the first traditions on fledgling Route 66—the Wun-Stop-Duzzit. That name, plus its Panhandle convenience in Amarillo, got the business off to a good start. It was often said that a traveler far from home always got the same price as a local buyer. But it was the owner's gift for capturing the imagination that spelled success. Cal Farley was a natural-born promoter. And he had nerve.

At a time when Amarillo's oil boom was dwindling, new tires weren't a high priority with folks on the High Plains. Yet Cal wanted to demonstrate the clear superiority of the BFGoodrich product he carried. He knew the tires were tough, but he needed to make new customers out of disbelievers. So Cal hired a pilot and chartered a sleek monoplane, ready to prove how rough and ready his tires were. In the press and on the radio, he announced that he would toss a mounted and inflated tire out of the airplane at an altitude of no less than 2,700 feet.

Now that would be a fair distance even for one of today's tires. In 1929, when tire failures were as common as table salt, they might as well be dropped from the moon. But Cal had faith in his product and carried on in the face of heavy betting that favored his opponent.

On the appointed day, at a field where a white target circle had been painted, dust rose from the cars—hundreds of them—that brought Texans from every direction to witness the event. Cal's chartered plane took off, and traffic on every nearby road stopped. Finally, after the plane had circled the field enough to be sure of everyone's attention, a mounted tire flew from the open doorway, heading straight down for the target. It hit with a smashing thump, bounced a couple of hundred feet into the air, and came to rest undamaged. Cal's point was made: These are really tough tires and we sell 'em. The *Amarillo Daily News* gave Cal Farley's promotional event most of the front page. Business soared.

To keep things moving right along, Cal also ran his own live radio show from the Wun-Stop-Duzzit and planned other stunts, like having his lowest-ranking salesmen ride donkeys in a parade through downtown.

But the Depression was deepening, times were getting tougher, and the number of abandoned youngsters on Amarillo's streets grew daily. Most had already been arrested for petty theft of food and clothing, and the rate of serious crime among young boys was rising.

If others could ignore the problem or postpone it with jail sentences, Cal could not. He knew kids from his days as a baseball player, he understood their needs and their fears, and he knew something needed to be done. But it had to be more than a momentary stunt. Somehow these kids had to be unplugged from their city-street lives and given a fresh start out on the land. Cal Farley labored and hustled and jawboned.

And in 1939, on the steps of a crumbling courthouse in the ghost town of Old Tascosa, Cal Farley accepted on behalf of thousands of boys he would come to know, a grant of 120 acres to be called Boys Ranch. The first staff members came from Elk City, Oklahoma. The boys came from everywhere. Three youngsters were even put on a bus by their destitute mother with tags that read "Deliver to Boys Ranch, Amarillo, Texas." A movie was made by MGM. The boys kept coming.

The Wun-Stop-Duzzit eventually became a department store with the same reputation for variety and fairness as the original Route 66 business. And Boys Ranch is still going strong, with an additional 3,000 acres and close to 500 residents.

There are other stories of love and wisdom to be found along the old highway, but none with greater accomplishment.

NEW MEXICO

When weather can't seem to make it all the way east to Texas or Oklahoma, it just naturally drops in on Tucumcari. In fact, that's how the town got started in the first place.

At the turn of the century, two men were stranded at Six Shooter Siding by a mean-spirited three-week snowstorm. After a round of true hospitality, they just happened to mention that a railroad would be coming through. Land was snapped up, and when the railroad made Six Shooter Siding a regular stop, Tucumcari was born. Twenty-five years later Highway 66 was routed along that same railroad easement and Tucumcari became the town of a thousand motel rooms.

With Route 66 bringing carloads of people into Tucumcari every day, there was bound to be a mystery or two. The most baffling turned out to be the Matchbook Murder, ultimately solved by the sheriff of Quay County, Claude Monkus.

In 1951, a body was found by an itinerant bottle-picker three miles west of town. Yet there wasn't a single clue about who the victim was or how he came to be there. Only that someone had taken the trouble to shoot him five times.

Through fingerprints, Sheriff Claude located the victim's family in Ohio and obtained a description, along with the useful information that the man had been headed for California. Shortly thereafter, the victim's car turned up on an impound lot in Amarillo, bereft of any other clues, but bearing a matchbook from The Hitching Post in Sturgeon Bay, Wisconsin.

Armed with only that much, the sheriff began tracking the victim and his killer. After checking in with every gas station and motel as far east as Shamrock, he finally obtained a description of a hitchhiker seen in the victim's company. And sure enough, the owner of The Hitching Post recognized a former fry cook from Sheriff Claude's telephone description and remembered that the fellow quit to head for California.

An all-points bulletin went out on the murderer and some months later a young deputy in Northern California's redwood country arrested him. The trial in Tucumcari was brief, the verdict was guilty, and the matchbook murderer paid the price.

Sheriff Claude later received an award from his fellow peace officers in the tristate area, and in 1965 was honored as Peace Officer of the Month by *Master Detective Magazine*. No computers, no technicalities over DNA samples, just good old-fashioned police work and a single matchbook found along Route 66.

Wilmer and his sidekick Woofie were inveterate watchers. In fact, there were probably none better in the state of New Mexico. The two lived just west of Santa Rosa and always turned out to watch one of the state's two or three snowplows whenever a blizzard rolled in. And they measured carefully the progress of any roadwork.

So when Route 66 was finally graded and paved west of Santa Rosa toward Albuquerque, the boys had something special to scrutinize. A great deal of watching was needed, too, especially around Tijeras Canyon, which had stumped road builders for years. The route through the canyon to Albuquerque was torturous, with so many rock outcroppings to be cleared that the blasting went on for months.

Not long after they began serious watching of the blasting work—from an exceptionally safe distance—Wilmer and Woofie noticed something about the way in which the highway was being built. Instead of the steel forms they'd seen on another job or two, the Route 66 crews were using wooden forms nailed up from two-by-tens.

What's more, and this was the interesting part to Wilmer and Woofie, the wood was being constantly replaced with new stock. Around nightfall, as the job shut down, used two-by-tens were stacked neatly by the construction shack, later to be loaded onto a flatbed truck and hauled away.

Back at their cabin, Woofie opined that the Tijeras job was using a hell of a lot of new two-by-tens and that the old stock was certainly going somewhere. Wilmer agreed and the two invested in a long-distance telephone call to the Bernalillo County highway office. Were there any other construction jobs nearby to watch? No, nothing more than repair work. Sorry.

The boys thanked their informant, gave the long-distance operator the rest of their nickels, and figured they were definitely onto a profitable item. Winter would be coming on soon and they had no stove wood, except for some green piñon that smoked something terrible and put out precious little heat.

But they did have a good cross-buck saw that could cut through any of those two-by-tens in nothing flat. With a little hatchet work, they'd have enough stove kindling to last until the end of February at least.

Next morning Woofie and Wilmer skipped their usual breakfast at the White Cottage Cafe and headed straight for the job site. There they spent most of the day making sure they knew who the players were. Wilmer was pretty sure that the fellow standing over by the shack—who never got his hands dirty and nodded a lot whenever any of the crew spoke to him—was the foreman. But they wanted to take no chances by asking. So they put in another two days of watching, just to be sure.

At last they made their move. Sidling up to the foreman, Woofie began passing the time of day. It was hard going, too. The old guy was intent on the job and not very talkative. Woofie's chatter didn't seem welcome. So Wilmer, always the man with a friendly word, stepped in and went to work on the foreman. Once in a while, one of the construction crew would drive by in a truck giving a wave.

And all three men would wave back. By day's end, Wilmer
and Woofie felt like they were part of the crew.

Things progressed fairly well after that and Woofie
picked up a pint of expensive sour mash whiskey for the
foreman—as a token of friendship, you might say. Apparently he'd even got the right brand, because the foreman
seemed quite pleased by the gesture. Another day and
another pint, this time from Wilmer, and the time seemed
right to pop the question. Would anyone mind if they
stopped by tonight and picked up a few of those two-by-
tens?

The foreman said nothing, just stared at the frosted
ground, shaking his head slightly. Woofie knew instantly
that they had come up short and beat a hasty retreat, leaving Wilmer to put a little friendliness back into the nego-
tiations. In due time, Woofie was back with a whole fifth
of the very agreeable sour mash whiskey.

That certainly seemed to do the trick. Another word
or two and the foreman nodded. Sure, nobody would notice a few missing two-by-tens. Help yourselves.

That night Wilmer and Woofie had piled nearly all the
wood into an old pickup with bad springs when a deputy
sheriff rolled up in his black Ford. This time the negotia-
tions were short and sweet. Woofie explained that they
were just unloading a bunch of two-by-tens—as a personal contribution to the good work being done by the
road crew. It's our patriotic duty, Wilmer told the deputy.

Woofie was more straightforward. He wanted to know
if it was the booze-guzzling foreman who'd ratted them
out. The question puzzled the deputy. As it turned out,
he'd just happened by with no crime fighting on his mind
at all. And the foreman? Well, the deputy explained, the
job's foreman was down with the crew supervising all the
blasting, just like always.

Then who was that fella up by the construction shack?
And that put a stitch into the deputy. Between belly laughs
he told the pair that the old guy they'd been buying sour
mash whiskey for was another sidewalk supervisor—a
full-time watcher just like themselves. Wilmer and
Woofie were so stricken by the news that the deputy told
them to keep some of the two-by-tens still on the pickup.

Hell, someone else was stealing them anyway.

For earlier travelers on Route 66 through the Southwest, the only continuing fact of life other than the highway itself was the Santa Fe Railway. On a two-lane where hours of solitude could pass without the sight of another vehicle or even a line of telephone poles to mark the distance, there was little contrast or relief from creeping boredom. Especially for backseat kids.

Oh, there were the steep-sided arroyos along the highway, where a sign reading DIP marked the point at which the family car would become completely airborne at any speed over 55 miles per hour. Those were always good for a little excitement.

The rest of the traveling day was quartered into times when the silver-sided Chief or Super Chief came tearing through. Hitting over 90 miles per hour on some straight stretches, the Santa Fe streamliners in their red, yellow, and silver color schemes hissed by at such a rate that passengers' faces were only a blur.

But if each train encounter was a major event of the day for Route 66 travelers, the streamliners also marked the end of a lucrative trade in Indian blankets carried on at depots across the West. By the late 1940s, the trains were stopping in fewer cities, and then only briefly. Not enough time for passengers to appreciate the wares or to buy.

Soon the blanket merchants moved on over to roadside souvenir stands along Route 66. It wasn't the same, though. One Navajo woman, who worked with her weaver-mother outside the Fred Harvey Alvarado Hotel in Albuquerque, remembers that train passengers were more considerate and less inclined to haggle over small amounts than tourists on the highway. She also recalls how Anglo merchants at the depot began hurting the trade by hiring Pueblo Indians to sell cheap blankets—made in Brooklyn—for much less.

For a time, the daughter tried to even the score by telling customers that the competition sold blankets that were transported by diseased people. That's why the goods were so much cheaper. When her mother learned of this, she was both angered and amused, so the girl was scolded in good humor. Nevertheless, machine-made blanket sales increased and the Navajos soon moved on.

For years, all that remained of their presence was the little Navajo boy whose image appeared in Santa Fe advertising. In the end, even that disappeared as an undesirable stereotype, along with the passenger service of which the Santa Fe Railway was once so proud.

West of Albuquerque, along the older 32-mile stretch of highway from Los Lunas to Correo, there was little action other than double-headed Santa Fe freights and the railway's sleek streamliners. The rest was and still is New Mexican arroyos, scrub, and sky. So travelers were more than ready for a stop at Dan's Bar, Cafe, and Motel. And they often got more than they expected.

Dan's was one of the original last-chance operations. Except in place of two-headed rattlesnakes, the place featured a midget bull and Katy the Dancing Bear. Although it was true that Katy could do a few steps, her real interest lay in hustling the tourists for drinks, and she was very good at it. Some even said that Katy could read the labels, because she clearly knew the difference between soft drinks and beer—which she would always choose at any distance, and could drain faster than a chugalug champ.

This same section of Route 66 was also a favorite haunt of New Mexico state policemen who needed relief from a relentless desert sun and the loneliness of patrol. In the 1950s, just before Correo was bypassed by the new Albuquerque cutoff, Dan's was also a hotbed of illicit competition between the highway patrolmen, who were running pursuit-model Fords, and Dan's employees, who favored the hot new Buick Century. Somehow, when they caught sight of one another on a straight stretch, the checkered flag just naturally dropped, with the Buick going two for three. Though the participants were never found out, you could always tell from the smell of burned oil coming from a pair of cars parked out front—along with windshields made opaque by sacrificial bugs—that the boys had been at it again.

Correo is gone now, with virtually no remains. But if

you listen for the sound of racing exhausts on the wind and keep an eye out for official muscle cars, you won't be disappointed. Hot police vehicles may still populate this stretch of highway, driven by officers of the court, no less, looking for a little action out on Route 66.

Not many along old Route 66 knew of the Singing House. Fewer speak of it today. It is one of those stories of the heart that could suffer at the hands of strangers and is not often repeated. But there is a spot, hidden from view, west of Laguna and north toward the Continental Divide, and it is there that the house once stood.

No one knows exactly where the builders came from. Somewhere near Fort Smith, Arkansas, they say: a hard-working but frail man and his handsome wife, driven out by the dust and hard times of the 1930s. Picking up Route 66 in Oklahoma City, the couple made it to Santa Rosa before their ancient Willys gave out. It was too expensive to fix, so they traded it for a clapped-out Reo and struggled into Albuquerque before it too died a junker's death.

The wife, it is said, had a voice as sweet as sunlight on the dew. She'd sung since her school days at a country church and had even been approached by talent agents. But she wanted nothing to do with the commerce of music.

Still, when the last of their money was gone and her husband was ill from walking the city in search of an honest day's labor, the wife had a change of heart. Dressing in her best, she went from one place to another until she found a club owner who would hear her. As the club's small band fell in behind the simple melodies she sang, the room hushed. Her voice, with its transparent quality, compelled attention and sold extra drinks. The club owner knew a voice of gold when he heard it and hired the woman on the spot.

Soon she had become the most popular singer in the valley. Yet, even with more than enough money to move on, her husband recovered slowly. He was, you see, not working. And that fact sapped whatever strength he found in himself.

The clear New Mexico air agreed with him, though, and his color was better than his wife could remember.

He'd also taken up whittling again, rendering in soft, piney detail the small desert animals he'd seen along the edges of the city.

So one Sunday morning his wife said what was on her mind. Why not build a home in the high country just to the west? He was handy and could do much of the work himself. She could finish out her scheduled performances and help him. Perhaps they could even find a market for his carvings. Surprisingly, her husband took to the idea and they found a perfect building site, plus two workers from the Pueblo who were wizards with adobe.

Nearly every day, as the work progressed, the wife would sing to her husband and the workmen and to the house itself while she labored alongside them. When the house was finished, the sound of her voice seemed to have become a part of every brick and board. Indeed, in the afternoon breezes, windows opened on opposite sides of the house brought a sweet trilling that rose and fell, changing its timbre with the wind. Neighbors from small homesteads nearby heard of the house and often stopped by just to hear its song. The man and his wife were obliging but not encouraging. It was a private thing, they felt.

With their house safely up before the first winter storm, the husband drove off one morning with samples of his work to show owners of souvenir shops along the highway. He was more confident now; everyone who'd seen his carvings wanted to buy and his work would surely sell well once the Depression ended. With a snug house and a great many of the husband's carvings put by, they looked forward to a bright future.

Accounts differ about what happened next, of course, as accounts always do. Some say the wife was trying to save her husband's carvings from a flash fire that engulfed their home. Others say the fire was set by intruders. There was no real evidence one way or the other. The husband knew only that his wife had perished, and after a few disconsolate weeks, he wandered off alone, disappearing without a trace.

Only four sentinel corners of adobe bricks remain. Even the charred roof timbers have been carried away for firewood.

Yet here is a strange thing. Occasional visitors to the

site swear that the sweet voice embodied in the house can still be heard. Inexplicably, it is clearest on a day when there is no wind at all. The almost transparent tones do not come, it is said, from the adobe pillars, nor from anything that can be found in the ruins. The soft trilling is simply there, in the clear New Mexico air, just above the rock and weathered grasses. As if it had always been so, here along the great spine of America's West.

Crooks never had much of a chance on Route 66 through the West. Many, from scam artists to killers, traveled the road, but little crime was actually committed along its path. That's not due to any gentling effect of the highway, however.

Instead, the low crime rate was because most towns only had one major thoroughfare—Route 66. It's the way into town and the only way out. No choice of north or south or back-alley places to hide. Commit a crime here, stay here.

In Gallup, Nechero's Texaco station has been robbed only once in fifty-three years of service to Route 66 travelers. Gallup is too small to hole up in, and once you're out of town there's just nowhere to go. Faced with the Great Empty to the west, one crook raced back into town, only to be stuck behind the Inter-Tribal Indian Ceremonial Parade. When the parade passed by the police cruiser at the far end of town, the cops simply pulled the robber from his car and tossed him in the clink.

The parade itself has always been held on a Saturday in August, and it's a three-hour lulu. It is such a big deal, in fact, that when Highway 66 was first routed through Gallup, a special exemption was required. You see, US numbered highways were supposed to remain open, no matter what. But not in Gallup. Here, the parade came first.

It took a while for federal and state planners to accustom themselves to that idea, but they finally took it gracefully. And for over six decades, traffic halted on Route 66 while dancers, drummers, riders, and townspeople celebrated the Native American heritage to which the town owes a large part of its culture, art, and livelihood.

Today New Mexico has a well-deserved reputation as a moviemaking center. Hollywood productions began making films in Las Vegas twenty-five years before Route 66 made an appearance, when crews and equipment traveled only by train. Las Vegas boasted excellent rail connections. The city also offered first-rate accommodations for cast members at Fred Harvey's La Castaneda Hotel, with a pretty fair nightlife to boot.

Albuquerque also managed to attract a little of the movie action in those early years. But the biggest burst of moviemaking energy was centered in Gallup. And not by accident. Stars of the 1940s and '50s like Errol Flynn, Spencer Tracy, Virginia Mayo, Robert Mitchum, Gene Tierney, and Kirk Douglas were in part lured to Gallup by a well-appointed watering hole that was already legendary among Hollywood's elite—El Rancho Hotel.

The place was comfortable enough for Mayo's entourage and spacious enough for Flynn, who typically rode his horse right on through the lobby and straight into the bar. Even today, the place holds an uncanny power of attraction.

El Rancho's rooms are also named for the stars who stayed in them. And therein lies a grand tale. At a time when Hollywood had a reputation for wild parties and outrageous behavior, studios were unwilling to acknowledge that two of their top stars were even traveling together, much less romantically involved. Of course, gossip columnists had been busy linking Spencer Tracy—quite accurately, as it happens—with Katharine Hepburn.

When location work on *Sea of Grass* was begun in Gallup, it was carefully announced through the press that Tracy and Hepburn were not present. Yet many recall seeing them together around El Rancho at the time, and the rooms still bearing their names are right next door to one another. So where does life end and legend begin?

Mike Pitel of the New Mexico Tourism Department wondered the same thing. So he did a little undercover research at El Rancho, figuring that Spencer and Kate were getting by, despite pressure from studio executives. Perhaps even after all these years, there still might be a clue.

There was. When Pitel and a fellow investigator

rented the Tracy and Hepburn rooms for a night, they discovered—in the farthest reaches of a closet along the adjoining wall—a flimsy hardboard panel tucked in place and easily removed. This was all that separated the two rooms. El Rancho had gone the distance to aid in the triumph of love over public relations.

Historically, Western New Mexico and Northern Arizona have been competitors. But the people of both states were united in helping the Dust Bowl refugees headed west. In a steady stream they came, Okies mostly, but Arkies and Georgia crackers too—their land broken or just plain gone.

On they came. For those who'd begun the journey with old trucks and cut-down cars, the grades beyond Albuquerque took their toll. Ruined hulks of the refugees' pitiful machines were scattered all along Route 66, as were their unmarked graves.

Roadsiders generally had little more than the refugees themselves. Some merchants even conspired to sell spoiled food, faulty auto parts, and bad tires. Even tap water carried a price often beyond measure. Gas was a few cents a gallon. Water for a thirsty infant could run fifty cents a pint. So Dust Bowlers learned to take their water from the creek beds. Free—until some black-hearted people began poisoning the waters.

By the mid-thirties, countless thousands of those on the road knew they had no hope at all of getting through on their own. Everything that had ever been theirs was gone—except for relentless hunger.

But when certain starvation faced the travelers, people along the roadside pitched in with everything they could find. Tourist courts in New Mexico gave free clothing and food to children. Doctors along the border delivered and mended as best they could, buying medicine on what little personal credit they had left.

This outpouring of love is one of the most remarkable things to come out of that period, gracing Route 66 in a way nothing else could. For long after the thin trails of homeless families had crossed into California, the refugees remembered their debts. When there was finally enough to make it through each day, they began sending what they could to the people who had helped them. In the form of nickels and dimes and worn half-dollars, it was sent— month after month—to the Samaritans of Route 66.

Today there is still a small society of families made up of the families of roadsiders and the refugees they befriended. A bond spanning sixty-some years still connects those long-ago travelers with people from Grants, Thoreau, Gallup, Lupton, Allantown, Holbrook, and Winslow. Letters and snapshots taken by their children of new grandchildren are exchanged, and holidays are spent together as human kindness during those terrible times is still honored.

ARIZONA

Unlike some towns along the highway, Winslow has little in the way of local curses and doesn't want any. It is often difficult enough to accomplish something here without interference from the netherworld. Townfolks work hard, take their pleasures as they can, and keep track of the traffic on Route 66. Sometimes that's plenty.

In fact, the only occasion when traffic was halted on Route 66 occurred in the 1940s. A local pub owner faced the problem of moving his solid thirty-foot bar across the highway to a new location. The bar had been custom-built right inside Bus & Bill's Bar, so it would be a shame to break it up just for a trip across the street.

Yet, as the bar stood—huge, cumbersome, and glued to the floor by its own tonnage—no moving company would touch the job for less than a second mortgage. At length, after everything else had been moved, Bus put out the word: Grand Closing! Free Beer at 4 P.M. Sharp! Small boys circulated a stack of handmade posters among the town's most cost-conscious elbow-benders.

An offer of free money couldn't have attracted more able-bodied regulars in this parched high-desert community. At the appointed hour, Winslow's stoutest menfolk stood shoulder to shoulder along the heavy wooden structure at Bus & Bill's. And after several rounds, Bus announced his intention. The bar would now be moved across the street.

Bus's patrons gave it their best. Holding longnecks in one hand and a length of bar in the other, they all faced north, grunted, lifted, and strained. The bar, now looking like a crippled mahogany centipede of monstrous proportions, wobbled slowly through the front door and out onto Route 66.

But the need for relief was evident, so Bus made another announcement. It was definitely time to take a break. And the moving crew had certainly earned it. With a great, scraping *crumph,* the bar teetered and came to rest in the middle of America's busiest transcontinental highway, bringing traffic to a complete stop.

The din made by horns of cars and trucks must have been deafening. But the boys would not be hurried. Another round of free beer was served and amiably discussed. Finally, accompanied by sounds of pure-malt satisfaction, the bar made its way to the other side of the highway.

Some years later, as the story still circulates around town, many have expressed an interest in preserving the moment. A small memorial plaque was considered for a time. But the best suggestion was to place a standard yellow-diamond caution sign at the spot. In honor of one of the few times Route 66 was ever closed to traffic, the sign would read: SLOW! BAR XING.

Travelers along Route 66 have always been well regarded by towns and businesses along the way. But the turkey award usually went to the big-city tourists—demanding types who sneered at local customs.

Still, Route 66 can be a great equalizer, and for many easterners, the trip west could be arduous off the road as well as on it. Some roadside businesspeople, especially on slow days, were even known to lay in wait for the self-absorbed and incautious. One who did was the concessionaire at Meteor Crater.

Rimmy Jim ran the combined trading post, chat-and-chew filling station, and liquor store that bore his name. A former cattle baron who'd been run to ground by rustlers over the years, Rimmy Jim had learned to take life one day at a time, usually accompanied by a heavy dose of humor.

With a ten-gallon hat that he wore with the fore brim turned down like a dress fedora, Rimmy Jim played a novel hybrid role that was part cowboy, part Ernest Hemingway.

Locals loved the show, and from his vantage point on the crater rim, the canny shopkeeper carefully watched the cars out on Route 66. When someone whose car he recognized didn't stop for coffee when headed up to Flagstaff in the morning, he'd charge them double when they stopped in for a cup on the way back. And over the years, he kept up a series of running gags with just about everyone in the region.

Rimmy Jim had only two sore spots: salesmen and snooty eastern ladies. He dealt with the salesmen by offering to bury them free if they even stepped foot in his place. Most, seeing the wild look in Rimmy Jim's eye, skedaddled without leaving their automobiles. The fact that there were some headstones randomly placed just out back probably hastened their departures.

Rimmy took a little more time with eastern female tourists, however. It was a long way between rest stops in those days and people often drove in just to use the facilities.

There was some primitive indoor plumbing for paying customers at Rimmy Jim's place. But when he spied an ample lady with eastern airs, Rimmy invariably sent her on to the outhouse several yards removed from the storefront. Once the lady had time to be firmly ensconced there, a voice from a hidden loudspeaker would issue from the recesses below the seat.

In pleading tones, Rimmy would ask the woman to move over to the second hole since he hadn't finished painting the underside of the first one yet.

Most everyone in Northern Arizona was in on the joke, and locals would often drop by just for the regular sight of matronly forms exploding from the outhouse door in total disarray.

There are plenty of rest stops and trading posts along Route 66 these days, and Meteor Crater is still open for business. But there will never be another place like Rimmy Jim's. All those who knew him regret the passing of that time and of what he brought to the highway and all those who loved it.

There's not much left at Two Guns, just east of Flagstaff. And it is wise not to explore there today. That may be just as well. For the place is also said to be cursed, with death or financial disarray in store for anyone who occupies this place.

The sorry history of Two Guns began with the slaughter of fifty Navajo men, women, and children by Apache raiders from the White Mountains to the east. After a second raid, the Apaches vanished, but were later discovered by Navajo trackers to be hiding in a cave at Canyon Diablo, the present-day site of Two Guns. Caught in their underground hideout, with no chance for escape, the Apaches were eventually smoked to death by fires set at the cave's entrance by the Navajos. Since then the site has been considered sacred by both nations. Only a few outlaws ever frequented the place, and to a man, they got their tickets punched by pursuers.

By the time a forerunner of Route 66 spanned formidable Canyon Diablo in the early 1920s, a lodge and post office had been established—this despite Indian warnings that warrior spirits roamed the canyon, often in the form of mountain lions. The property owner was one of many who ignored those warnings and never lived to reap the bounty from tourists he'd planned on. In 1926, when Highway 66 was officially routed through Two Guns, he was brutally murdered and his store burned to the ground.

Now you'd think that plans to commercialize the death cave would die with him. But a new owner turned up and pressed on with the project. Again ignoring Indian warnings, he cleared the cave of its relics and used the skulls of the fallen Apache warriors as decorations.

Then, in the ultimate nose-thumbing, he built cages out behind his gas station and there put captured mountain lions on display to the tourist trade. Within months, the would-be showman was clawed and nearly cut in half by two of the creatures. Shortly after that, his daughter was killed in a freak accident on the highway, and the man left for good.

Two Guns opened and closed again several times over the years, but the site was too attractively situated on

Route 66 to stay empty for long. Another owner stepped in, and for a time it did quite well. But in 1971 the place mysteriously blew up. Everything was destroyed, except the lions' cages and a few rock walls.

A newer gas station and campground, off the original site, have since opened and closed. And in the early 1990s, another new owner took possession, had impressive color photographs of himself taken, and promised great things for Two Guns. He even put up a small fee to have the curse lifted, but the Indian medicine man knew he was being underpaid by a wealthy promoter and left the curse in place. After a series of unhappy incidents, the new owner put the place up for sale.

If you're a betting person, the odds favoring history are now about eight to one—except throughout this area, you'll find no takers on either end. Dark is dark and better left alone.

One of the last towns along Route 66 in Arizona to catch the fever of highway revival, Flagstaff is now solidly aboard. And the Museum Club has been a leader in preserving the mood of the road's glory days.

Formerly called the Zoo Club in deference to all the animal heads hung on its walls, the place recalls the while-you-wait taxidermist who originally practiced here, and predates Route 66 by over a decade.

Built in 1915, the exterior has changed very little over the years and is a testament to log construction. Inside, the club is pure wild-west saloon, with an arched bar and supporting pillars furnished by the five trees around which the place was built. Indeed, if Annie Oakley and Teddy Roosevelt got together to design a bar, this is what it would look like. Absolutely bang-bully.

The club has had its share of fame and misfortune, too. Although it gained an early reputation as a playpen for local rowdies, it was later transformed by a new owner. Live music became the mainstay, with the likes of Waylon and Willie playing here, along with assorted local bands.

Everything was looking up when the owner's lovely dark-haired wife fell to her death from the club's staircase. The owner took his own life soon after.

Exactly the stuff of ghost stories, right? Yep. The club has since had several encounters of the harrowing kind, but none of these centered on the double tragedy as might be expected.

Instead, the accounts are of a young blond woman with crystal-green eyes who has been appearing or making her presence felt here since the late 1950s. Over the years, the woman has ordered drinks, only to disappear; lit wood fires in the great hearth after closing time; and left chairs rocking in the empty club. Moans of pleasure have also been heard in a vacant upstairs apartment.

Credibility has been added to these reports by a live-in manager who was actually pinned to his bed—control your fantasies here, guys—by the blonde, who clearly intended him anything but harm. That manager bailed out of a second-story window, rolled down the roof below, and still shaking, called the present owner from a nearby pay phone. Pausing only to clothe himself, he left town and hasn't been seen since.

So who could this wandering spirit be? Just another disembodied soul, with no connection to Route 66 or the club? Seems unlikely, doesn't it? After all, whatever spirit world exists would certainly be governed by certain natural laws, however unfamiliar to us.

Ghosts, like their physical counterparts, do not appear randomly in the universe. Some, bent on a trip along Route 66, might have migrated here with no trouble at all. If you happen to be in the Museum Club around closing time, you may have cause to consider the possibilities.

For now, it is enough to speculate about what the lady might prefer in the way of a drink. An extra glass ordered at a secluded corner booth? Sure, why not?

During World War II, a gunnery school for bomber crews was located right along Route 66, near the site of the present airport, east of Kingman. Some of the wartime structures are still there. After the war, Kingman's base became one of the first aircraft boneyards. As Storage Depot 41, the field took in bombers and fighters from everywhere. At one point, over 7,000 surplus aircraft were dumped here by the War Assets Administration. Finally, someone asked what was going to be done with it all.

At first, the government tried to sell the aircraft off singly or in small lots. But there aren't a lot of uses for B-17s and dive bombers in peacetime, and the scrap aluminum market was more than depressed by the surplus—it was nonexistent. Mind you, B-25 bombers were even being flown in with full tanks, straight from the factories still producing them after the war's end.

All of which prompted a local businessman to step forward. He offered to take all that junk off the government's hands and melt it down for little more than his cost. The government, nearly desperate in a political year, even helped out with a grant, wondering, no doubt, where the fellow's wits had gone.

Not long after, a routine inspection tour by federal auditors revealed our entrepreneur's secret. He was indeed handing off the scrap metal for virtually nothing—but he was making a fortune by selling the aviation gas left in the fuel tanks of every arriving aircraft.

And you were wondering how toilet seats could possibly cost the government several thousand dollars each . . .

During the early part of World War II, with terrible losses for America in the Pacific, everyone's attention was on survival. Survival in combat, survival of relationships, survival while crossing the country—the desert, especially—with worn-out cars, bald tires, and heavily rationed fuel.

Yet for one courageous young bride, the highway offered the shortest, perhaps only, route to her husband's side. An Army Air Corps pilot, he was assigned to a special new task group, to be formed at a base in Florida. After the briefest of honeymoons, he flew directly to a top secret base in Florida.

Many road maps were both poor and outdated, with no new printings and most of the cartographers drafted for military duty. It was the same with the highways themselves—little or no maintenance and detours appearing everywhere, some for the duration.

So the bride did her best. It was vital that she see her

new husband again before the war took him away. She tried to call several times, to let him know she was coming, but communications with the new group were blacked out.

Setting out from the West Coast, she followed Route 66 as far as Oklahoma City, then continued east through Fort Smith to Eglin Field in Florida. But by the time she arrived, the group had already been transferred to another base and everything was totally hush-hush.

Wives have a way of knowing when the chips are really down, and the young bride kept her spirits up in the face of no news at all about her husband or his group's mission.

The news finally broke early in 1942. Doolittle's Raiders had flown army bombers off the aircraft carrier USS *Hornet* and bombed Japan, our first effort in turning the tide. Her husband had been one of the badly wounded pilots, but he survived. Their story later became part of an MGM movie about the raid and its effect on the crew's lives.

The young bride was Ellen Lawson and her husband was Lieutenant Ted Lawson, pilot of the seventh B-25 in Jimmy Doolittle's raid and subject of the best-selling book and a film, *Thirty Seconds Over Tokyo*. Later, a town on Route 66 in Missouri renamed itself Doolittle, in honor of the raid's leader and the courage of all the men who took part.

It's often the fashion of some of today's top writers to make a show of themselves and their work. Yet the granddaddy of all Route 66 authors was not like that. Though he later received both the Pulitzer and Nobel prizes for literature, John Steinbeck remained unassuming, private, and passionate about his work. He also cared deeply for the migrant workers he knew from his own days of laboring in the fields.

Virtually no one recalls the author's passage along Route 66 before writing *The Grapes of Wrath* in his Los Gatos, California home. Taking notes of as many as 2,000 words a day—in longhand—he traveled the highway, patiently building the basis of what would become the Joad family's flight westward. In his journal, Steinbeck later lamented his work, believing it was not very good. A run-of-the-mill book, he thought, though the world soon came to know better.

Arizona sections of Route 66 appear during a montage sequence in John Ford's film production of Steinbeck's masterpiece. And shots of the highway along the California border give great depth to the feeling of being on the road during those Dust Bowl days.

Along the Colorado River shore at Needles, where the temperature is often at epic highs, is a place where Steinbeck waded into the river to escape the heat. Later, realizing the power of giving oneself to the waters, the novelist wrote of the Joad menfolk doing the same thing. It is a simple moment in the story, yet Steinbeck's compassion and his plain words help confer humanity upon all of us.

CALIFORNIA

It is in the nature of a free people to take much of their independence for granted. Which leads us to complain about the federal government and the justice system from time to time. Both are flawed, of course. So are we all. It comes with the territory.

But the Great Depression of the 1930s still reminds us that freedom is always subject to the personal fears of those in power. It can disappear in a flash. And even if recovered, it can be a hard thing to get people to talk about afterward.

Take, for example, our freedom to cross state lines whenever we wish. We think nothing of such freedom today. Yet during the Depression, it was a close-run thing—especially along the California border.

You see, California more than any other state was cut off by its mountains and deserts from the rest of the country. That continued until well after World War II. Simple things like cars and major appliances were manufactured within the state because transportation costs from the East were too high. Long-haul trucking was almost unknown, and the Santa Fe Railway had but a single track along its right-of-way. That's one of the reasons Hollywood film sets had a special look to them—no one recognized even simple appliances like the telephones. They were designed and produced on the West Coast. And the resulting cultural gap exists to this day.

During the Depression, with so many displaced people headed west, away from worn-out land and a busted industrial economy, the power brokers of California grew nervous, and as the flood continued, became frightened silly. What would happen if all those people discovered the truth: that the ranchers and labor contractors were in cahoots to drive the wages of all farm workers down by ensuring an oversupply? What then?

So a little money and a lot of political influence went looking for the weakest link in the moral chain. And it turned up at command levels in the Los Angeles Police Department.

Over the years, the LAPD has had more than its share of rogue chiefs. Even potential reformers were bent by the power that comes with running a police force that ranked in size as the fifth largest army in the world. In the 1930s, the force of that power was brought to bear at California's borders.

Meanwhile, sheriff's departments worked with railroad bulls to keep newcomers from coming by riding the rails. They certainly accounted for their share of mayhem. But it was the LAPD that overstepped every legal boundary. Squads numbering fifty heavily armed officers were sent to the state's borders on every highway. Their orders? Turn back, by lethal force if necessary, anyone with less than a hundred dollars to show. Which turned out to be almost everybody. None of the officers could boast of a hundred bucks in their pockets. Yet that was the test for migrants, for any traveler.

Using agricultural inspection stations, bridges, or anything at hand, these men established barriers to free travel along the borders of not only Arizona and Nevada but Oregon as well. Not that the other states minded at first—until refugees who were turned back became another state's problem.

In the end, it took undercover federal marshals to break up what California newspapers called "the bum blockade." And even then, the brutality and outright murder did not stop. Cities and counties simply hired local toughs to man the barricades and to burn out refugee camps wherever they could. Borders remained closed and the final death count will never be known.

Today as we sail down the highway, confident in our right to go wherever we please, it's worth a moment to reflect on the price paid for our freedom by thousands of plain people whose only crime was the crushing burden of survival in a broken land.

West of the Cajon Pass, Barstow and Victorville stand like sentinels in a region, where distances are so vast that life even along the main road is risky and difficult. Even the desert towns found on maps are not towns anymore. Most began life as section camps for the railroad, retaining their alphabetic names when the highway was built. Amboy, Essex, Fenner, and Goffs now barely exist, though if you say the names quickly they give the impression of an expensive law firm.

Undoubtedly, it was the sparse population of these towns and the surrounding desert that gave rise to a truly horrifying construction plan for the Route 66 corridor in this region. Picture this: Some Atomic Energy Commission physicists are sitting around Washington back in the late 1950s. They're trying to come up with new ways to justify the enormous cost of nuclear power—and their own jobs—to the American public. Plus which, they have a bunch of surplus atomic bombs sitting around Albuquerque, taking up shelf space.

The cold war was on, of course, and in the race for weapons superiority it was important to use up the old stuff that no one knew how to get rid of, especially the high-radiation bombs that could leave any detonation site uninhabitable for half a century or more.

An idea occurs to the physicists. Why not move mountains with them, like for a new highway or something? And what better place to try this out than on the Great Mojave Desert. Remember that these are very dirty bombs, and the AEC guys are not exactly right-brainers—the desert is nothing but dirt to them anyway. If it all goes sour, where's the harm?

Enter the California Department of Transportation: highway builders in a state where more goofy ideas find the light of day than anywhere else on earth. High-level discussions are scheduled over the idea. A low-profile public relations effort is begun. Trial balloons are sent up. And at last a full proposal is presented. California's Atomic Highway nears reality.

As documented, the joint plan called for no fewer than twenty-two full-scale nuclear weapons to be planted along a two-mile stretch of intended roadway through the Bristol Mountains. The destructive power of these bombs will be 133 times greater than the force of the two atomic weapons dropped on Hiroshima and Nagasaki. The purpose and effect of these buried devices would be to vaporize every mountain in their path.

But where would all that radiated vapor go?

Why, right into the atmosphere, of course. The blast was expected to produce a primary dust cloud reaching a minimum altitude of 12,000 feet, with a diameter of over seven miles from ground zero. Of course, the resulting bang might shorten the route by almost fifteen miles. Golly, who wouldn't want that?

Incomprehensibly, the plan went forward as officials from the federal government, Santa Fe Railway, and Caltrans were busy deciding where to put the reviewing stand and VIP seating. There is no record of anyone giving thought to the consequences of the blast for people living in nearby communities. But the officials did have their reviewing-stand decorations all picked out.

In a rush of good sense, the Russians saved our bacon by unexpectedly signing the 1963 Nuclear Test Ban Treaty. That agreement stopped a whole lot of insanity right in its tracks. But the image of all that radiation released by American scientists on life in our own desert lingers. It is more than a little troublesome.

Hamish McGill—we'll call him that—paid his taxes, cherished his family, and never had a single brush with the law. At least not until the state of California told him that a new highway cutoff would cross his property. Even then he did his best to accommodate the highway men. They could put their highway here or there, just so long as it didn't separate his livestock from the only source of water.

Now, the truth is that civil servants often lose sight of what they're about. The words *civil* and *servant* lose all meaning when small-minded—some might say pea-brained—officials get puffed up with themselves. The highway men realigned their proposed roadway, all right. The new alignment not only threatened the McGill family's livelihood but would pass right through their house.

Hamish resisted. He slipped on his small square spectacles every night to study the law governing rights-of-way in California. The highway men were wrong and he cited chapter and verse to Sacramento. The highway men reacted by having McGill's entire ranch condemned, sending the sheriff out with an eviction order.

Hamish resisted again. So the sheriff swore that McGill and his whole family had assaulted a duly sworn peace officer. He sent deputies out to arrest everyone on the property, including the family dog if they could find one.

Hamish resisted yet again, and after what passed for a trial, he was sent off in leg irons to do ten years' hard time in a Northern California prison. An older immigrant to this country, Hamish took separation from his family very hard, but he kept his nose clean in prison where, being the only literate, bespectacled prisoner, he ran the library and earned his con name, Four-Eyes.

By the time they let Hamish McGill out he was nearly sixty years old, his wife had died, and his family had scattered. But Hamish was not one to get angry when he could get even. He landed a job as a janitor with the same state of California that had taken his land and ruined his life. He kept his mouth shut and read every bit of paper in every trash basket he emptied.

By 1932, Four-Eyes McGill knew where every piece of livestock owned by the California Highway Commission was kept, when they were moved, what they were fed. And he knew exactly how they were branded—with a stylized CHC.

A year later, Hamish McGill left his job, bought a large truck, and set up shop on the high desert, just off Route 66 near Adelanto. His first incursion behind the highway

commission's fencing netted him a very fine team of
mules, with which he graded several long double-ramp
pits. These were located not far from remote grazing
lands and were deep enough to hide his livestock truck
from view, even in daylight.

From then on, it was a piece of cake. McGill knew
horseflesh and could still spot a good side of beef. So he
kept up his unauthorized transfers of highway commission
stock until his personal record of what the State of California owed him was balanced out—with interest added
at 6 percent for the time he had served in prison.

As his livestock interests grew, Hamish steadily moved
them over to a little spread off Route 66 in Arizona.
There the locals found him to be an honest and friendly
neighbor, running a fine herd—under his own Four-Eyes
brand.

On the original alignment of Highway 66 that wound
through downtown L.A., the route passed right by a
Southern California legend: Ptomaine Tommy's. There
are several well-known burger shacks around town that
echo the name of the old beanery, now long gone. But
the original Ptomaine Tommy's was an institution unto
itself.

Back in the late 1920s, Tommy's—nobody called it
Ptomaine's—was a booming business. And although the
twenties roared a lot less in Los Angeles than in Chicago,
the restaurant was a favorite after-hours hangout for West
Coast gunsels, movie people, and the local literati. F. Scott
Fitzgerald hurled his lunch in Tommy's regularly when he
was in town working on a screenplay. No reflection on
Tommy's food, though. Fitzgerald was a champion drinker
of everything in sight.

What really pulled 'em into the joint was not Tommy's
celebrity status, but the food. Stars and mobsters of that
period shared one characteristic: they loved to indulge
themselves at low cost. And Tommy's provided big por-
tions at rock-bottom prices. In fact, low prices were what

allowed Tommy's to survive and reach stardom on its own—thanks to the Great Depression.

Tommy's had always offered a version of chili con carne. But in true California fashion, it was only a burger topped with chili beans from a small ladle. Still, the customers liked it and double orders at 30¢ each were common. Then the Depression really kicked in. Even movie stars had little more to spend than drifters, and at Tommy's it paid to know the code.

In this case, the code was "chili beans, con carne size." That meant the hamburger patty would be the same, but a larger ladle was used for the chili at no increase in price. Soon the item was simply listed on the menu as chili size. It only cost a dime back then, but you can still order its namesake all over the West. So if ever there is to be an official Route 66 dish, let it be the chili size.

Of all the intangibles associated with travel along Route 66, the image of Hollywood was one of the most compelling. If you had a promise of work there, so much the better. If not, maybe you'd be discovered. Maybe right along Route 66, on Santa Monica Boulevard.

Sometimes it actually happened. Sometimes the studio machine scooped up a Margarita Carmen Cansino (Rita Hayworth) or a Norma Jean Mortenson (Marilyn Monroe) and made them stars. But mostly Hollywood was and is a place where something terrific could happen. That was perhaps its greatest attraction to someone headed west.

In the heyday of Route 66, of course, Hollywood was far more prominent than it is now. Motion pictures were produced on the huge sound stages around town. But all that effort was also invisible. Almost no one got onto the lots who didn't work there, and something like the Universal Tour was unthinkable. Hollywood was so totally self absorbed that another city almost stole the famous name right out from under it.

The truth was that most movies were made in Culver City, home of companies like Metro-Goldwyn-Mayer, derived from Ince and Sennett's first studio. And, as it happens, Hollywood is really not a city at all. Most of it is part of Los Angeles; some is in unincorporated areas of the county. Knowing this, and having been rebuffed by studio officials in a 1937 attempt to gain recognition for themselves, the Culver City council went right for the jugular. With no public discussion, they passed a resolution that officially changed their city's name to Hollywood.

Well, Los Angeles practically had a cow, and the squabble went on for months as crosstown moguls tried to use the issue to settle old personal scores. Finally the Selznick studio worked out a compromise. City fathers from both sides got together at Grauman's Chinese Theatre, a few blocks north of Route 66. There, alongside the stars' footprints in the forecourt, they ceremoniously buried a movie-prop hatchet. The hatchet is still there and so is Hollywood.

Capitol Records, whose disc-and-stylus tower still dominates the skyline above Route 66 in Hollywood, was a success right from the beginning. And no one was more responsible for Capitol's early rise in the recording industry than Nat King Cole.

Nathaniel Coles followed his sweetheart to L.A. in 1937. He was only nineteen but had a knack for keyboard styling, and was soon pioneering a brand-new sound in jazz with a drummerless combo of piano, rhythm guitar, and bass.

By the mid-1940s, the King Cole Trio had a string of solid hits. But in the winter of 1946, history swerved slightly to include a chance meeting that would bring new glitter to the Cole legend and guarantee legendary status for Route 66.

Nat was wowing an upscale crowd at the Trocadero on Sunset Boulevard. Along with Ciro's and the Mocambo, the Troc ranked as one of the most influential nightclubs in showbiz. So if you made it at the Troc, the world was your oyster.

The King Cole Trio was making it, but the schedule was a killer: straight sets from early evening until two in the morning—close to eight hours each night. Several new records were also in the offing, but Nat had yet to find a good B-side for one of the numbers to be recorded in

March. It was already February. Time was short and not much new material was surfacing.

But it would. Oh boy, how it would! For a young Philadelphia songwriter was heading west in his green Buick convertible. Bobby Troup was a former Marine and an eager beaver, with a seventeen-week hit of his own, "Daddy," to recommend him. But it had been recorded five years earlier. Bobby needed something new, kicky, jivey. Something cool to audition on the West Coast. Route 66 gave it to him.

Only a day or two into the trip west, Bobby was already searching for a lyric that had a little sizzle. Lyrics for "Route 66" began running through his head. The thing was, he might have only one shot. Bobby was armed with a new swing-blues number to audition called "Baby, Baby All the Time"——and an enterprising Hollywood agent who knew the right people. He took Bobby to the Troc.

After the last set, the agent managed to fast-talk a fatigued Nat Cole into a five-minute listen. As chairs in the King Cole Room of the Troc were being stacked atop the tables, Bobby sat down at the piano, and in his nervousness, fell backward off the stage.

There have been better openings to a crucial audition, but as Bobby ran through the sultry chording and lyrics of "Baby," the song connected. Nat was impressed and asked for more, catching Bobby completely off guard. So the young songwriter came back with the opening of his Route 66 tune. It was only a fragment, a few bars. It was also enough.

Nat knew the jump-blues beat would work. He'd already had success with that formula. Besides, Nat knew Route 66——the roadside diners and sagebrush motels of that two-lane ribbon from Chicago——a whole lot better than most; he'd driven it himself a dozen times. A recording date was coming soon and this could be the side he'd been searching for. When could Bobby have it finished? Tomorrow? No. A week, then? Done.

Next day, barely unpacked, Bobby checked in at the recording studio just a few blocks off Route 66 in Hollywood. In a practice room, he spread out a US map above the piano keyboard, tracing the route as the litany of towns came back to him. Oklahoma City, Amarillo,

Gallup, Flagstaff, eye-blink Winona—had to have a rhyme for Arizona—and on west to San Bernardino. Place names and the road beat began to fall together, ending with a bit of jive talk.

Nat introduced the song at the Troc as soon as the lead sheets were ready. A few weeks later, the Trio recorded several numbers and broke for lunch. The session had gone well and everyone felt that they were greasing it. In that mood, Nat and the Trio returned to cut "Route 66." One of the most memorable road songs ever recorded was done in just one take. Everyone in the studio knew the performance was flawless and the cut was good.

But no one, especially not composer Bobby Troup, knew then how good the song was, or what an enduring hit it would become. The tune stayed on the hit parade for two years, and thousands of westbound travelers used it as their only road map. The song and the highway became part of the national consciousness. Route 66 had arrived.

Bing Crosby would do it next, with the Andrews Sisters. And over the intervening years, Bobby's song would be recorded by performers as diverse as Mel Tormé, Bob Wills, the Four Freshmen, Chuck Berry, the Rolling Stones, Van Morrison, Charles Brown, Manhattan Transfer, Michael Martin Murphey, Asleep at the Wheel, and Depeche Mode.

Even as Route 66 itself was being decertified as a US highway by transportation officials, the song rolled on. In succeeding generations, there will surely be more pressings of the classic. But it was done first and certainly best in Hollywood, just a stone's throw from the highway itself.

Santa Monica is nestled snugly between the well-manicured lawns of Pacific Palisades, and the freer lifestyles of Venice, making the city a culturally neutral terminus for old Route 66. Santa Monica was named not for the saint herself, but for two blue pools of fresh water that reminded an early missionary of that good lady's tearful eyes.

Since then, Saint Monica has become more generally known as the chief inventor of body guilt. But that reputation has little effect on the performers at Muscle Beach to the south or the exclusive tanning salons just to the north.

As with many city sections of old Route 66, those crossing Los Angeles and Santa Monica are not typical of the roadside images we carry of the highway in more open places. Yet the stories are often just as good.

Anyone approaching the beach after nightfall in the late 1930s was treated to an entrancing sight. For just beyond Santa Monica Pier was one of the major attractions—or eyesores, depending on your viewpoint—a full-on gambling ship. And the presence of that offshore beacon of sin, gloriously lighted by night, gave some locals fits. It was probably less a matter of moral outrage than the fact that no one ashore was getting much of a cut. The ensuing squabble led to the infamous Battle of Santa Monica Bay.

The *Rex,* strung fore and aft with lights totaling over a million candlepower, was the dreamboat of one Tony "The Admiral" Cornero. And it must be said right up front that Cornero was not your ordinary gangster. Tony found smuggling too rough and got out of that racket right after he'd made his first million. Thereafter he concentrated on entertainment-style gambling, drawing some 13 million players—at a time when Las Vegas was no more than a wide spot on dusty desert highway.

In the end, the presence of the *Rex* and Cornero's profits became just too much for the supply-side thinkers of the day. Restaurateurs were annoyed by Tony's free buffets; studio heads felt he was muscling in on their entertainment business. They began howling about moral impropriety, and Attorney General (later US Supreme Court Chief Justice) Earl Warren was pressed to serve notice on Cornero.

That notice was ignored, as were others, and in 1939 an unlikely assault force made up of state, county, and local cops headed for the *Rex* in a bobbing flotilla of water taxis commandeered from the Santa Monica Pier.

Cornero was surprised by the tiny squadron but not unprepared. He had machine-gun emplacements on the ship's cut-down mastheads—in case any of his mob friends planned to pull a heist—but had given strict orders to his men not to fire on the lawmen.

The law boats, commanded largely by officers who were themselves regulars at the ship's tables, knew the faces behind all the gun sights ranged above them. They also knew that the raid was a joke and began slipping close enough to the *Rex* to accept complimentary bottles of brandy passed down by friendly crew members.

After nine hours of circling, everyone except Earl Warren—who was trying with little effect to direct his flotilla by telephone from Sacramento—felt that justice had been sufficiently served. With raucous farewells that could be heard on shore, the assault force withdrew. Not a shot had been fired. Not a single lawman had stepped aboard Cornero's *Rex*. The Battle of Santa Monica Bay was over.

Hollywood executives, cut out of the action aboard ship, nonetheless got a piece of the Cornero pie. *Mr. Lucky,* a film starring Cary Grant in a gambling-ship story, was released in 1943. And a television series of the same name, loosely based on adventures aboard the *Rex*, aired in the late 1950s, with a memorable score by Henry Mancini. Both shows did well financially as the green of Hollywood envy changed to the shade of money.

And Cornero? Far from Route 66, in the Nevada Desert, he later put together his biggest deal: the Stardust Hotel and Casino, among the first of the great draws on the Las Vegas Strip. But with irony even Hollywood couldn't top, Cornero suffered a massive heart attack and fell dead on a gambling table.

He was down ten thousand bucks.

POSTSCRIPT

Traveling Route 66 is an intensely personal experience, but never more so than here at the ocean's edge. From my very first family trip west, Route 66 has always had some influence on my life. While still a youngster—staying in West Los Angeles just a block off Route 66—I discovered some busy home-style neighborhood restaurants, each with its share of solitary regulars.

We all turned up at about the same time every evening, and I sometimes shared tables with two great storytellers who became heroes of mine. One was Rod Serling; the other was Paul Brinegar. A native of Tucumcari, Brinegar attracted little attention in his hometown, but returned years later starring as the crusty old trail cook Wishbone in the television series *Rawhide*.

Most of the show was shot near Tucumcari. It was an ideal location for a make-believe cattle drive and Paul had plenty of stories to share with a kid back in L.A.—like which members of the cast couldn't ride a horse for squat, which were the biggest party animals, and which kept young-and-tenders scattered among Tucumcari's one thousand motel rooms. All pretty juicy stuff.

Those stories are blurry now, but I do have a clear memory of a cast member Paul brought along to dinner one night. The young actor's in-your-face manner, coupled with a sandy voice that was both soothing and unnerving, made me agree with Paul that from any distance this guy was star material. In fact, I still have an old eight-by-ten glossy that he sent along later. The photograph is signed: Clint Eastwood.

The end of the road is also a reminder of the emotional distance Route 66 covers on its way from the Heartland to the West Coast. In the balmy morning air, a tan silver-haired woman in her sixties strolls sweetly down Ocean Avenue in a beaded jeans jacket and well-tailored denim miniskirt. She has great legs and wears the outfit perfectly—bringing it to life as she walks by.

Two young men leaning against a red Alfa Romeo

follow her every movement with their eyes. She acknowledges them with a smile and they resume their conversation. On the rear of their car is a bumper sticker. Without apology, the sticker reads: JACK NICHOLSON FOR GOVERNOR.

Ah, California, where everything is still possible.

ROUTE 66 MILEAGE TABLE

Wondering whether to keep going or stay put in the motel you found with great neon and magic fingers? Here's a quick estimator. Cumulative mileage appears in the outside columns for both westbound and eastbound travelers.

Point-to-point distances on Route 66 appear as the first number in the center column. Comparable interstate distances are shown in parentheses. Where no number appears, it means the interstate is not close by or there is no measurable section of Route 66.

All mileages shown here are the result of averaging corrected odometer readings with distances given in AAA publications and official state DOT maps, so the numbers may not exactly match a map you are using. But for all sources taken as a whole, any differences will be as small as possible.

WESTBOUND READ DOWN		EASTBOUND READ UP
0	Chicago, IL	2278
	40 (42)	
40	Joliet, IL	2238
	59 (64)	
99	Pontiac, IL	2179
	36 (40)	
135	Bloomington, IL	2143
	31 (32)	
166	Lincoln, IL	2112
	31 (31)	
197	Springfield, IL	2081
	46 (44)	
243	Litchfield, IL	2035
	55 (44)	
298	St. Louis, MO	1980
	64 (60)	
362	Stanton, MO	1916
	48 (43)	

410	Rolla, MO	1868
	63 (58)	
473	Lebanon, MO	1805
	57 (51)	
530	Springfield, MO	1748
	72 (77)	
602	Joplin, MO	1676
	35 (24)	
637	Miami, OK	1641
	64 (55)	
701	Claremore, OK	1577
	28 (23)	
729	Tulsa, OK	1549
	52 (50)	
781	Stroud, OK	1497
	60 (52)	
841	Oklahoma City, OK	1437
	27 (26)	
868	El Reno, OK	1410
	52 (59)	
920	Clinton, OK	1358
	43 (40)	
963	Sayre, OK	1315
	31 (32)	
994	Shamrock, TX	1284
	31 (28)	
1025	Alanreed, TX	1253
	67 (64)	
1092	Amarillo, TX	1186
	47 (46)	
1139	Adrian, TX	1139
	65 (64)	
1204	Tucumcari, NM	1074
	64 (58)	
1268	Santa Rosa, NM	1010
	77 (58)	
1345	Moriarty, NM	933
	37 (34)	
1382	Albuquerque, NM	896
	74 (46)	
1456	Laguna, NM	822
	30 (31)	

1486	Grants, NM	792
	32 (30)	
1518	Thoreau, NM	760
	31 (33)	
1549	Gallup, NM	729
	49 (48)	
1598	Chambers, AZ	680
	50 (48)	
1648	Holbrook, AZ	630
	— (32)	
1680	Winslow, AZ	598
	— (46)	
1726	Winona, AZ	552
	17 (14)	
1743	Flagstaff, AZ	535
	40 (31)	
1783	Williams, AZ	495
	43 (45)	
1826	Seligman, AZ	452
	62 (—)	
1888	Hackberry, AZ	390
	27 (—)	
1915	Kingman, AZ	363
	28 (—)	
1943	Oatman, AZ	335
	43 (—)	
1984	Needles, CA	292
	74 (80)	
2060	Amboy, CA	218
	80 (79)	
2140	Barstow, CA	138
	36 (34)	
2176	Victorville, CA	102
	29 (26)	
2205	San Bernardino, CA	73
	56 (54)	
2261	Los Angeles, CA	17
	17 (13)	
2278	Santa Monica, CA	0

END—WEST   **BEGIN—EAST**

INDEX